ADELPHI
Paper • 301

Conventional
Arms Control and
European Security

Contents

Oxford University Press, Walton Street, Oxford OX2 6DP
Oxford New York
Athens Auckland Bangkok Bombay
Calcutta Cape Town Dar es Salaam Delhi
Florence Hong Kong Istanbul Karachi
Kuala Lumpur Madras Madrid Melbourne
Mexico City Nairobi Paris Singapore
Taipei Tokyo Toronto
and associated companies in
Berlin Ibadan

Oxford is a trade mark of Oxford University Press

Published in the United States
by Oxford University Press Inc., New York

First published June 1996 by Oxford University Press for
The International Institute for Strategic Studies
23 Tavistock Street, London WC2E 7NQ

Director: Dr John Chipman
Deputy Director: Rose Gottemoeller

British Library Cataloguing in Publication Data

Data available

Library of Congress Cataloging in Publication Data

ISBN 0-19-829241-4
ISSN 0567-932X

INTRODUCTION

Despite the collapse of the Berlin Wall in 1989 and the dissolution of the Soviet Union in 1991, the West is still seeking to develop an effective security system to replace the confrontation of the Cold War era. In doing so, Western strategists have three primary objectives. First, the West must forge a relationship with the Russian Federation that emphasises cooperation instead of confrontation. This will depend on a proper balance between Russian and Western security concerns, on the direction of continuing change within the Russian Federation, and on maturing relations between Russia and the former Soviet republics and between Russia and the former Warsaw Pact states. Second, an effective European security architecture must not only resolve conflict, but also assist in preventing conflicts, such as in the former Yugoslavia. Third, as this security structure evolves, every effort should be made to maintain NATO unity. While the transatlantic relationship will not remain static, it will, for the immediate future, continue to be a basis for European security and stability.

Throughout the Cold War, arms control was an important instrument in managing East–West competition and preventing superpower conflict. Arms-control negotiations fell into three main areas: conventional, nuclear and chemical or biological. Conventional arms talks resulted in the ratification of the Treaty on Conventional Armed Forces in Europe (CFE) in 1992, and the Confidence and Security Building Measures (CSBMs) initially agreed to in 1986 under the auspices of the Conference on Security and Cooperation in Europe (CSCE – now the Organisation for Security and Cooperation in Europe, OSCE). These agreements sought to reduce the risk of surprise attack, assist in crisis management, remove disparities prejudicial to security, establish lower force levels for conventional armaments, expand the East–West dialogue on military affairs, and strengthen stability throughout Europe.

Some argue that conventional arms control has little value in a post-Cold War environment characterised more by cooperation than confrontation, and there is no doubt that the end of the Cold War has dramatically changed the geopolitical context of all arms-control efforts in Europe. If the critics of future efforts are to be challenged, new initiatives as well as current accords must be examined, evaluated against the developing security environment, and modernised where necessary. Failing to do so will render such agreements irrelevant and sacrifice the advantages they offer, particularly in limiting force numbers, providing information exchanges, increasing transparency and allowing for intrusive verification.

It is important, however, to distinguish between 'arms control' and 'disarmament'. 'Arms control' refers to agreements between two or more states to limit or reduce certain categories of weapons or military operations to diminish tensions and the possibility of conflict. It also includes measures to verify compliance and enhance transparency. 'Hard' arms control refers to reductions or limitations of actual military hardware, while 'soft' arms control is normally associated with transparency measures over military exercises, budgets and doctrine. 'Disarmament', by contrast, is often imposed by a state or group on one or more states, normally at the conclusion of a war, such as the limits imposed on Germany at the end of the First and Second World Wars, or the restrictions placed on Iraq by the United Nations at the conclusion of the 1991 Gulf War. This distinction is important because while an arms-control regime is maintained by a harmony of interests among the participants, disarmament may require external pressure to ensure implementation and compliance.

This study explores the future role of conventional arms control in enhancing European security. Chapter 1 briefly examines the history of conventional arms-control negotiations and agreements to determine the political basis necessary for their success. The agreements currently in effect, such as the CFE Treaty or the OSCE's CSBMs, form a foundation and a momentum for future arms-control efforts. The Treaty on Open Skies, although still pending final ratification and entry into force, may also play an important role in the future. It could support a new security environment, assist in the final resolution of compliance difficulties in other arms-control arrangements, or even be used as part of an overall arms-control effort in areas such as the former Yugoslavia. In this context, it is important to examine the contents of each arms-control agreement, the process that resulted in its adoption, and the prospects for its continued relevance. Multilateral negotiations like the CFE Treaty or the CSBMs tend to be 'unruly', requiring agreement to be reached by a large number of countries, often with disparate interests and agendas. Since even the wishes of the United States will not always prevail in future arms-control discussions, it is valuable to look at the process by which these agreements are maintained.

Chapter 2 focuses on the implementation of the CFE Treaty and its prospects. The process of implementation from July 1993 to November 1995, and the problems that still remain unresolved, are extremely relevant to an understanding of arms control and the future that it may have in Western strategy. The CFE Treaty was initially designed to establish a level of equality between NATO and the Warsaw Pact. The dramatic changes that occurred in European politics between December 1988 and December 1991, however, altered the context of the agreement almost immediately. Many of its stated purposes were overshadowed or even overtaken by new requirements. CFE was critical in disengaging the two military blocs – NATO and the Warsaw Treaty Organisation (WTO) – that had confronted each other in Central Europe for over 40 years. It also played a crucial role in the peaceful demise of the Communist bloc, the retreat of the Soviet Army to the territory of the former Soviet Union, and the transition from the Soviet Union to the Commonwealth of Independent States (CIS). In July 1992, the Supreme Soviet issued a report stating that the Treaty was 'the only real instrument making it possible to prevent an arms race among the states of the Commonwealth'.[1] In addition, the CFE Treaty was instrumental in creating the security framework that allowed a united Germany to be accepted by its neighbours.

Chapter III discusses the May 1996 CFE Review Conference, possible future arms-control negotiations, and their relationship to evolving European security structures. The issues presented at the Review Conference reflect the political changes that have occurred during the implementation of CFE, and establish a direction for the future. This chapter also examines prospects for similar sub-regional arrangements and the arms-control aspects of the November 1995 General Framework Agreement for Peace in Bosnia and Herzegovina, otherwise known as the Dayton Agreement. Critical to this analysis is the role of the United States and the Russian Federation, as well as that of existing security structures.

In formulating future arms-control proposals it must be remembered that states have consistently used arms control as a 'method' to achieve the 'objective' of improved security. It is not an objective in itself. Conventional arms control cannot succeed when states are at war, and is of little use when they enjoy good relations. Furthermore, although any negotiation will focus on the details of the prospective agreement, the arms-control process should always be consistent with the direction of national – or alliance – security strategy. Arms control is a political activity and cannot be divorced from other aspects of a nation's security and foreign policy. It is affected by domestic events, by relations between states, and by the bureaucratic process of the participants. In this regard, progress in one arms-control forum may be influenced – positively or negatively – by the success or failure of other negotiations, previous agreements, and the political relationship between negotiating parties. It can either contribute to improving or deteriorating relations between states, or be the effect of a significant change in inter-state relations.

This is not to say that conventional arms control is merely a component of an overall policy or strategy. Some strategists have attempted to treat arms control and arms build-ups as functionally similar in the pursuit of security, but this argument for inter-changeability or substitutability is exaggerated. A successful conventional arms-control agreement in which all participants share the benefits of reduced tensions, such as the CFE Treaty, while often a mixed-motive enterprise, is fundamentally co-operative. It casts a very different light on the international system and near-term interactions among states than would a competitive programme or unilateral arms build-up.[2]

I. A BRIEF HISTORY OF CONVENTIONAL ARMS CONTROL

Conventional arms control is not a product of the nuclear age. For centuries, states have used it as a policy tool to improve their security, save money, or limit damage from conflicts. Most arms-control efforts in the last century sought to reduce or at least restrict forces, although some did try to restrain technological advances.

In 1899, 108 delegates from 26 countries met in The Hague to discuss armament, the laws of war and the arbitration of conflict. Representatives from the Russian Empire proposed a five-year moratorium on armament production, prompted largely by domestic economic difficulties. The Hague Conference also considered banning the use of balloons as platforms to launch projectiles or drop bombs, outlawing the 'dumdum' bullet, and eliminating any production of chemical weapons. During these discussions, the United States firmly opposed any restrictions on the size of naval forces, mainly because of its strong geo-strategic position and growing fleet. Subsequent discussions in 1907 involving 256 delegates from 44 nations accomplished nothing in the area of arms control, although some basic laws for conducting warfare were established.

In 1921, the Washington Naval Conference, officially known as the International Conference on Naval Limitation, convened. Nine nations took part, most notably the United States, United Kingdom, France, Italy and Japan. The agreement reached by the five major powers, the Washington Treaty, is interesting for several reasons. First, it was asymmetrical, allowing Japan, France and Italy smaller forces than the United States and the UK. Japan, for example, was only allowed 60% of the capital ships allocated to the US and UK. Second, in accepting the Treaty, Japan was largely reacting to domestic economic concerns. Third, the Japanese military strongly opposed the agreement on the grounds that it was not in the interests of Japan's national security. As a result, the imperial government was eventually forced to exceed its stated allocation, and the Japanese government formally terminated its participation in 1936.[1] Curiously, the Washington Treaty only restricted capital ships. It did not consider the qualitative impact that submarines or aircraft carriers would have in future warfare, and contained no verification procedures.

These early arms-control efforts differed from initiatives since the Second World War as they were primarily a reflection of idealistic theory, and focused solely on reducing weaponry. Yet several conclusions can be drawn that are still pertinent today. First, self-interest and security are stronger motivations for states to seek arms control than altruism and a desire for peace. Arms control has been used by states as a way of enhancing their security by reducing the possibility of war, the level of violence should conflict occur, and the amount of defence spending necessary in peace time. Economic difficulties have frequently prompted states to seek arms-control agreements.

Second, the state of a nation's civil–military relations is crucial, both in acceding to arms-control agreements and in complying with them. The United States Navy successfully opposed naval arms control in preparation for both Hague Conferences, and the Imperial Japanese General Staff forced its government to renege on the naval agreements of the 1920s.

Third, conventional arms control is normally conducted in a multilateral forum, particularly in Europe. Since the various players calculate their security requirements and threats differently, reaching a consensus can prove difficult. Multilateral negotiations also involve the participants' political and economic institutions as well as their militaries. The results of arms-control talks must satisfy domestic constituencies, improve general security, and be consistent with agreed alliance strategy.[2]

Lastly, criteria that establish parity in armaments are essential to any negotiations. The specific military resources at issue in a conventional arms-control negotiation are complex components of a nation's total military capability, and no two nations' armed forces are structured in the same way, either in terms of weapons or of organisation. These asymmetries in formations and hardware complicate establishing parity of conventional forces.[3]

The Mutual Balanced Force Reduction Talks and the CSCE
In 1973, after roughly 25 years of Cold War confrontation, the United States and Soviet Union initiated both the Conference on Security and Cooperation in Europe and the Mutual Balanced Force Reduction (MBFR) talks. The prelude to these two negotiations, and the subsequent agreements reached under the aegis of the CSCE, reflect an evolution in the East–West relationship. Both Western and Soviet leaders compromised on several contentious issues, both for reasons of alliance unity, and in response to domestic pressures.

The Soviet Union initially proposed a European-wide security conference in the late 1950s. Moscow's strategy was to entice the West Europeans to negotiations that would include all the Soviet

Union's East European satellites, but would exclude the United States.[4] The Soviet Union also wanted its borders established after the Second World War and its hegemony over Eastern Europe to be confirmed. The West rejected this idea as contrary to NATO's best interests. For the remainder of the 1950s and most of the 1960s, conventional arms control was absent from the agenda of East–West relations as the two sides steadily increased their military power. The Soviet Union was periodically occupied with unrest in its empire – for example in Hungary in 1956 – and the United States began its long involvement in Vietnam.

By the late 1960s, however, attitudes had changed, largely as a result of domestic pressures. In 1966, US Senator Mike Mansfield began to call for unilateral reductions in the US forces deployed in Europe. His proposal to the US Senate in January 1967 was supported by 42 other senators. In many ways, this was a catalyst for negotiations. Both the United States and the Soviet Union feared the impact that a large-scale unilateral reduction in US forces might have on their security. The Nixon administration feared what it might do to Western defences and the viability of NATO, while the Soviets feared that it might lead the UK and France to share their nuclear secrets with Germany, as well as leading to a large-scale increase in the German armed forces – the Bundeswehr – to compensate for the departing US forces.[5]

In response to the Mansfield initiative, NATO presented the results of a study group, 'Future Tasks of the Alliance', also known as the Harmel Report, later in 1967. The Harmel Report was intended to re-focus the strong currents that were running against traditional NATO security policy. The report stated that the Alliance's two primary tasks were:

• to maintain sufficient political unity and military readiness to deter an attack by the Warsaw Pact; and
• to seek a more stable relationship with the Eastern bloc that would allow underlying issues to be resolved.[6]

The Harmel Report encouraged *détente* between the superpowers, thereby establishing a basis for arms-control discussions.

These negotiations did not, however, begin for five years because of conflicts in other areas. In 1968, the Soviet Union and its Warsaw Pact allies invaded Czechoslovakia, crushing the so-called 'Prague Spring'. Tension in East–West relations increased dramatically, temporarily forestalling any attempt at negotiations. It also temporarily relieved the pressure to withdraw US troops unilaterally from Europe. In spring 1971, the Strategic Arms Limitations Talks (SALT) signalled the onset of *détente*. The political climate had warmed sufficiently for conventional discussions to move forward.

The Mutual Balanced Force Reduction talks began in October 1973. The West's initial proposal emphasised reaching a level of parity in troop strength with the East through asymmetrical troop reductions, because of the Warsaw Pact's overwhelming superiority in manpower and its ability to send reinforcements to the theatre more rapidly. The West proposed that in the first phase the Soviet Union should remove a tank army of roughly 69,000 of its troops from Eastern Europe. The United States would in turn withdraw 29,000 troops. Western analysis suggested that to reach an eventual common ceiling of 700,000 troops would require a reduction of almost three Warsaw Pact soldiers to one NATO soldier.[7] Soviet policy from the outset, however, was to preserve the political and military status quo and its advantage in conventional strength. Accordingly, the Soviets rejected the concept of asymmetrical troop reductions. Although accepting this initiative would have reduced the possibility of a surprise attack by either side, it might also have weakened Moscow's control over Eastern Europe.

In 1976, the West added a nuclear package to its proposal. This was known as Option III, and consisted of a one-time reduction in US short- and intermediate-range nuclear systems in return for a reduction in Soviet manpower.[8] This was in response to Soviet insistence that any reduction proposal focusing solely on troops (the Warsaw Pact's advantage) was unfair without an associated reduction in Western nuclear systems (NATO's advantage). The Soviets rejected Option III as inequitable, and it was withdrawn by NATO in 1979. Option III, which even many Western observers thought was ill conceived, demonstrates the difficulty of determining a state of agreed parity between forces that are organised and equipped differently, enjoy diverse geographic advantages, and follow disparate military doctrines.

At this point, the MBFR talks stalemated, largely because the Soviet Union was unwilling to accept significantly greater reductions in its forces and those of the other members of the Warsaw Pact to achieve parity with NATO. During the 1980s, however, several important precedents were established that were to prove fundamental to the next reduction forum – the CFE negotiations.

The Eastern bloc eventually agreed to reduce its forces to a common ceiling. This was a critical departure from the initial position that clearly sought to maintain Warsaw Pact superiority. Moscow also finally accepted Western data on NATO forces as valid.

MBFR will probably best be remembered, however, for what prevented agreement being reached. First, the Soviets had never accepted that the West's data on Warsaw Pact forces was correct, and consistently presented figures that characterised East and West forces as equal.[9] This was in part disingenuous, but it also revealed the inherent difficulty of limiting manpower in any agreement. Even if a definition of 'manpower' could have been found that was acceptable to all parties, verifying any agreement in which personnel was the primary item to be limited would have been very difficult. Furthermore, US and Soviet forward deployed forces had an important deterrent value that exceeded simple numerical comparisons. The two sides' capability to add reinforcements in times of crisis also differed considerably.

Second, the MBFR talks did not include all NATO and Warsaw Pact members, but focused on so-called 'Central Europe'. For the West, this encompassed the Federal Republic of Germany, the Netherlands, Belgium and Luxembourg. For the East, it included the German Democratic Republic, Poland and Czechoslovakia. Nations with territory or forces in this region were included as direct participants, and countries bordering the region were indirect participants.[10] Hungary's potential direct involvement was left undecided, and France refused to participate at all in the discussions.

Third, both sides exploited the negotiations in pursuit of long-term foreign-policy objectives. The Soviet Union sought gradually to weaken NATO and reduce the US presence in Europe as a means of intimidating the West Europeans. They also sought to limit the size of the West German Bundeswehr. Conversely, the United States used the negotiations to forestall Congressional efforts to reduce US forward deployed forces in Europe unilaterally, and as part of its attempt to reduce Soviet influence in Eastern Europe.

The CSCE also convened in 1973. These negotiations were in some ways a Western compromise with the Soviet Union in return for its participation in MBFR, as they closely approximated the Soviet suggestion in the 1950s for a European-wide security conference. The CSCE also embodied the concept of *détente* that had been enunciated in the 1967 Harmel Report as a Western objective. The

Concluding Document of the CSCE, the Helsinki Final Act, was signed on 1 August 1975 by the 35 participating nations (the United States, Canada and all European countries except Albania). The repetitive language on territorial integrity that appears in five of the Act's ten principles emphatically underscores the parties' intention to recognise as 'final' the borders established after the Second World War.[11] The Helsinki Final Act launched the so-called 'CSCE process' that called for balanced progress in three areas – often called 'Baskets 1, 2 and 3': security; cooperation in science, economics, technology and the environment; and human rights.

Basket One resulted in modest agreements on confidence- and security-building measures, frequently referred to as 'soft arms control'. These CSBMs were designed to reduce the 'dangers of armed conflict and of misunderstanding or miscalculation of military activities which could give rise to apprehension'.[12] The first of these was a commitment to provide 21 days' advance notification to all signatories of any military exercise involving more than 25,000 troops. It also encouraged voluntary notification of smaller military training events, major military movements, and the invitation of observers to monitor manoeuvres. The successful conclusion of this agreement was in many ways a concession by the Soviet Union, which had long insisted that restrictions on military activities could not be agreed on until troop reductions had first taken place. The Western position, in contrast, had always been to seek CSBMs before reductions. The adoption of the initial CSBM package established a process that has continued to evolve in subsequent Vienna Documents which increased the number of CSBMs between NATO and the WTO. These served as a precedent for, among others, the arms-control portion of the 1995 Dayton Agreement. The CFE Treaty was also negotiated within the framework of CSCE.

As part of the CSCE process, the Stockholm Conference on Disarmament in Europe (CDE) was established in 1984 to deal with other Basket One initiatives. In 1986, members agreed to CSBMs that required notification of exercises involving 13,000 troops, the mandatory invitation of observers from other participating countries to attend military activities above a certain threshold, the exchange of annual forecasts for all notifiable military activities, and on-site inspections from air or ground to verify compliance. This CSBM package was further amended in the 1991 Vienna Document:

• The number of troops involved in an exercise requiring advanced notification was lowered from 13,000 to 9,000.

- More observers were allowed to monitor military exercises.
- The number of exercises that a state could conduct was restricted.
- Members agreed to an annual exchange of military data on the location, strength and composition of ground and air-force units, as well as an annual exchange of data on military budgets.

Additional adjustments, including an agreement on the conduct of military forces, were added in 1994.[13]

These CSBMs were clearly consistent with the goal of reducing the potential for war in Central Europe. In addition, the level of transparency and confidence they established provided a basis for actual force reductions. Curiously, however, the CSCE may have made its most memorable contribution in Basket 3, human rights, which was added almost as an afterthought to the initial Helsinki Final Act. In many ways, Basket 3 gave the West, as well as dissidents in Eastern Europe and the USSR, an important policy tool, and human rights played a key role in the demise of the entire Communist political system and the eventual end of the East–West military threat.

The Conventional Armed Forces in Europe Treaty
On 10 November 1990, the CFE Treaty was signed after 20 months of negotiations between the members of NATO and the Warsaw Treaty Organisation. Arms-control experts on both sides had benefited from many of the technical difficulties that had made an MBFR agreement remote. All members of both alliances took part, and the issue of including personnel as a category to be restricted was quickly discarded.

The rapid progress made by the CFE discussions is perhaps best explained by the dramatic political changes that occurred after the Treaty was signed, particularly in the Soviet Union. Mikhail Gorbachev's leadership in Moscow established the political conditions that allowed the process to speed to its conclusion. This was clearly underscored in his December 1988 announcement at the UN of a unilateral reduction in Soviet forces from Eastern Europe. There is also little doubt that Gorbachev was motivated by growing economic problems throughout the Soviet Union, and a desire to close a perceived gap between Western and Soviet military technology. Consequently, while the MBFR talks did have certain conceptual flaws, such as attempting to limit manpower and to include tactical nuclear weapons, the primary ingredient for the success of the CFE Treaty may have been the desire on the part of political leaders finally to reach an agreement.

At its completion, then US President George Bush hailed the CFE Treaty as ending the 'military confrontation that has cursed Europe for decades'.[14] Despite the dramatic nature of this document, the large-scale reductions required, and the complex inspection regime it established, the conclusion of the negotiations was overshadowed by the end of the Warsaw Pact, the collapse of the Berlin Wall, and impending conflict in the Persian Gulf. Even these events paled to insignificance when the Soviet Union disintegrated the following year. As a result, many observers announced the imminent end of CFE. The London *Times*, for example, sounded a particularly distressing note when it announced that 'Europe's most ambitious arms control treaty risks becoming unworkable because of the Soviet Union's disintegration'.[15] Yet the CFE Treaty survived the early reports of its death, testimony both to its contribution to European security and to the importance participating states attached to it. The unprecedented changes in Europe did, however, delay its entry into force, and the Treaty was not provisionally applied until 17 July 1992. It became legally binding on all parties on 19 November 1992.[16]

The CFE Treaty runs to over 100 pages encompassing 23 articles, several protocols and two annexes, with several associated legally binding statements and political documents.[17] The Treaty limits five categories of weapons – tanks, artillery, armoured combat vehicles (ACVs), combat helicopters, and attack aircraft (all known as Treaty Limited Equipment or TLE) – on the European territory of the NATO states and those of the former Warsaw Pact (see Table 1). This area is frequently referred to as the Atlantic to the Urals (ATTU) and is further subdivided into five zones (see Table 2). Each alliance is limited in each of these zones to a certain number of each category of TLE.

Despite being negotiated in a multilateral forum, CFE is firmly rooted in the alliance formations of the Cold War – NATO and the Warsaw Pact – and, despite the dissolution of the Warsaw Pact, the bloc-to-bloc character of the Treaty remains. Each alliance has the following limits: 20,000 main battle tanks; 30,000 ACVs; 20,000 artillery pieces; 6,800 combat aircraft (excluding trainers, strategic bombers and transport aircraft); and 2,000 attack helicopters. In addition, no single nation may hold more than one-third of the total

Table 1: TLE Holdings in 1992 and CFE Limits in 1995[a]

Country	Tanks		Arty		ACVs		Hel		Ac	
NATO Group										
Belgium	362[a]	**334**	378	**320**	1,383	**1,099**	8	**46**	202	**232**
Canada	76	**77**	32	**38**	136	**277**	0	**0**	28	**90**
Denmark	499	**353**	553	**553**	316	**316**	12	**12**	106	**106**
France	1,335	**1,306**	1,436	**1,292**	4,387	**3,820**	366	**396**	695	**800**
Germany[b]	7,170	**4,166**	4,735	**2,705**	9,099	**3,446**	256	**306**	1,040	**900**
Greece	1,971	**1,735**	1,975	**1,878**	1,432	**2,534**	0	**30**	455	**650**
Italy	1,232	**1,348**	2,013	**1,955**	3,774	**3,339**	176	**139**	542	**650**
Netherlands	913	**743**	837	**607**	1,445	**1,080**	90	**50**	176	**230**
Norway	205	**170**	544	**527**	124	**225**	0	**0**	89	**100**
Portugal	146	**300**	354	**450**	280	**430**	0	**26**	92	**160**
Spain	858	**794**	1,368	**1,310**	1,223	**1,588**	28	**90**	178	**310**
Turkey	3,008	**2,795**	3,107	**3,523**	2,059	**3,120**	11	**103**	360	**750**
UK	1,159	**1,015**	534	**636**	3,206	**3,176**	389	**371**	750	**900**
US	5,163	**4,006**	1,973	**2,492**	4,963	**5,372**	349	**431**	398	**784**
Budapest/Tashkent Group										
Armenia	n.k.	**220**	n.k.	**285**	n.k.	**220**	n.k.	**50**	n.k.	**100**
Azerbaijan	134	**220**	126	**285**	113	**220**	9	**50**	15	**100**
Belarus	3,457	**1,800**	1,562	**1,615**	3,824	**2,600**	76	**80**	390	**260**
Bulgaria	2,269	**1,475**	2,154	**1,750**	2,232	**2,000**	44	**67**	335	**235**
Czech Rep	1,803	**957**	1,723	**767**	2,515	**1,367**	37	**50**	228	**230**
Georgia	77	**220**	0	**285**	28	**220**	0	**50**	0	**100**
Hungary	1,345	**835**	1,047	**840**	1,731	**1,700**	39	**108**	143	**180**
Moldova	0	**210**	108	**250**	98	**210**	0	**50**	30	**50**
Poland	2,850	**1,730**	2,315	**1,610**	2,396	**2,150**	30	**130**	509	**460**
Romania	2,967	**1,375**	3,942	**1,475**	3,171	**2,100**	15	**120**	508	**430**
Russia	9,338	**6400**	8,326	**6415**	19,399	**11,480**	1,005	**890**	4,624	**3,450**
Slovakia	901	**478**	1,258	**383**	1258	**683**	19	**25**	114	**115**
Ukraine	6,128	**4,080**	3,591	**4040**	6,703	**5,050**	271	**330**	1,648	**1,090**

Notes: [a] Initial number = 1992 holdings; bold number = 1995 holdings.
  [b] Includes TLE of former East German Army. Iceland, Kazakhstan and Luxembourg have no TLE in the area of application. Estonia, Latvia and Lithuania are not participants.

Sources: Dorn Crawford, *Conventional Armed Forces in Europe (CFE)* (Washington DC: US Arms Control and Disarmament Agency, 1995), p.7. See also 'Final Weapons Reduction Under the CFE Treaty', *Arms Control Today*, January 1996, pp. 29–30.

group entitlement for any category of equipment. CFE also requires states to place a specified portion of their allocation in designated permanent storage sites, and includes careful definitions of terms such as 'groups of parties', 'artillery' (which must be 100mm or larger) and 'designated permanent storage sites'. It further lists procedures for establishing a Joint Consultative Group (JCG), made up of representatives from every state party to the Treaty, to monitor problems that might occur during its implementation, proper methods of verification, periodic exchanges of information and to update definitions as new equipment types are deployed.

Both NATO and the WTO negotiated their respective national entitlements with their members abiding by the group ceilings and other associated requirements. The Warsaw Pact did so at negotiations held in Budapest in 1991. Following the dissolution of the Soviet Union at the end of 1991, the successor states agreed to their respective limitations at Tashkent on 15 May 1992. The division of Czechoslovakia into the Czech Republic and Slovakia on 1 January 1992 forced further adjustments to be made. Besides the revised totals for each emerging former Soviet state, two other official statements made by the Soviet Union – and later adopted by the successor republics – deserve particular mention.

The first, made on 14 June 1991, states that all TLE assigned to naval infantry or coastal defence forces counts as part of the total CFE Treaty entitlement. The West insisted on this to assuage concerns that the Soviet Union had transferred large amounts of equipment from the army to its naval forces to avoid Treaty obligations. The second statement acknowledged that the Soviet Union was required to destroy roughly 14,500 pieces of TLE that had been moved east of the Ural Mountains, and therefore outside the area of the Treaty, during the negotiations. The first statement is legally binding on the Soviet Union and its successor states, while the second is seen as a political obligation.

The CFE-1A discussions began in November 1990, shortly after the Treaty was signed, and focus on manpower reductions. Despite initial problems resulting from the dissolution of the Soviet Union, agreement was finally reached in July 1992. The resulting document, 'The Concluding Act of the Negotiation on Personnel Strength of Conventional Armed Forces in Europe', is not a treaty, but rather a political agreement under which the participating states undertake not to exceed the number of air, ground and naval personnel they have declared for the CFE area of application after March 1996 (the end of the CFE implementation period).[18]

Table 2: CFE Zones and Geographical Limits on States Parties

Zone[a]	Countries	Limits (Group)
4.1	All signatories' territory from the Atlantic to the Ural Mountains. (*Active Units*: Tanks:16,500, Artillery: 17,000, ACV: 21,400)	**Overall** Tanks: 20,000 ACV: 30,000 Arty: 20,000 Hel: 2,000 Ac: 6,800
4.2	*NATO Group*: UK, Portugal, Spain, France Italy, Belgium, Netherlands, Denmark, Germany, Greece, Norway and Turkey. *Warsaw Pact Group*: Czech Rep, Slovakia, Hungary, Romania, Bulgaria, Moldova, Georgia, Armenia, Azerbaijan, Ukraine, Belarus and Russia (to the Ural Mountains)	**Overall** Tanks:15,300 Arty: 14,000 ACV: 24,100 **In Active Units** Tanks: 11,800 Arty: 11,000 ACV: 21,400
4.3	*NATO Group*: UK, France, Italy, Belgium, Netherlands, Denmark and Germany. *Warsaw Pact Group*: Czech Rep, Slovakia, Hungary, Poland, Ukraine (former Kiev MD and North Carpathian MD), Belarus and Russia (Moscow and Volga-Ural Military District)	Tanks: 10,300 Arty: 9,100 ACV: 19,260
4.4	*NATO Group*: Netherlands, Belgium, Germany and Luxembourg. *Warsaw Pact Group*: Poland, Czech Republic, Slovakia and Hungary	Tanks: 7,500 Arty: 5,000 ACV: 11,250
5.1	*NATO Group*: Turkey, Greece, and Norway. *Warsaw Pact Group*: Romania, Bulgaria Moldova, Georgia, Armenia, Azerbaijan, Ukraine (former Odessa MD) and Russia (Leningrad MD and North Caucasus MD)	Tanks: 4,700 Arty: 6,000 ACV: 5,900

Note: [a]The zones are commonly labelled in this manner (i.e., 4.1, 4.2, etc.) after the paragraphs in Articles IV and V in which they appear.
Source: Crawford, *Conventional Armed Forces in Europe*, p. 9.

Treaty on Open Skies

In addition to the CFE Treaty, the NATO states, former members of the WTO, the Russian Federation, Belarus, Ukraine and Georgia signed the Treaty on Open Skies on 24 March 1992. Negotiations on this accord began in 1989, and it is based in many ways on a concept first proposed by President Dwight Eisenhower in 1955. This Treaty covers the entire territory of all signatories, and other members of the CIS or OSCE may also accede to it. The Treaty's main objectives are:

- to promote greater openness and transparency in military activities;
- to improve the monitoring of current and future arms-control provisions;
- to strengthen crisis prevention and crisis management; and
- to provide for aerial observation based on equity and effectiveness.

Each state shall accept, and may conduct, observation flights on the territory of the other signatories. An Open Skies Consultative Committee will decide on the quota of flights for each state party on an annual basis.[19]

The Treaty was designed to enter into force 60 days after ratification by 20 states. While it was hoped that this would happen fairly rapidly, the Treaty on Open Skies has languished in the parliamentary process in several countries. It was ratified by the United States and all of its NATO partners in 1994, but is still awaiting a vote in the Russian Duma. With Russian presidential elections looming in June 1996, the Treaty is unlikely to be presented to the Duma before autumn 1996, and its prospects are not good. The Ukrainian parliament voted on the Treaty in January 1996, but it did not receive sufficient votes to pass and a second vote will be scheduled. Final implementation of the Treaty on Open Skies would enhance transparency among the participating states and might help resolve one of the remaining problems of the CFE Treaty, the status of the equipment moved east of the Urals by the Soviet Union. Although there is no direct link between the CFE and Open Skies agreements, using Open Skies to determine the status of the Soviet equipment east of the Urals would be consistent with one of the objectives of Open Skies to facilitate the monitoring of existing arms-control agreements. It could also be used – perhaps in a modified form – to enhance transparency in the former Yugoslavia. In this context, discussions on the principle of aerial observation might be important, even though establishing a regime might take some time.

II. CFE IMPLEMENTATION AND PROSPECTS

The amount of equipment allowed and the geographic limitations imposed by the CFE Treaty, while important, are only a technical reflection of the strategic goals of both NATO and the Warsaw Pact when the CFE negotiations commenced. The Treaty's mandate describes these goals clearly. They include:

- strengthening stability and security in Europe by creating balanced conventional forces;
- establishing lower levels of conventional armaments and equipment;
- eliminating disparities prejudicial to stability and security; and
- precluding the capability for launching surprise attacks or large-scale offensive operations.[1]

These goals in turn clearly illustrate traditional conventional arms-control objectives – they reduce the risk of war; limit damage if war occurs; and lower the costs associated with military forces.

Despite the tremendous changes in Europe since 1990, the CFE Treaty continues to foster these goals and remains in the best interests of all parties for several reasons. First, the stabilising limits mean that no participating signatory can exceed its limits in any category of forces or increase its CFE-limited arsenal without both the concurrence of the other members in its group and corresponding reductions by one or more states in its group. Consequently, the Treaty has reduced the possibility of both arms races throughout the continent, and of a surprise attack by one state (or groups of states) on another. It also gives Hungary the means with which to constrain an expansion by the Romanian military, and Turkey a mechanism by which to limit and monitor Greece – and vice versa.[2] Second, the CFE Treaty enhances conventional deterrence by expanding the 'transparency' of each state's military forces, thus reducing the possibility of accidental conflict. Third, the Treaty requires notification of any change in the size and character of the participating states' military forces and an annual exchange of information. It further requires states to inform all signatories when their TLE will be modernised. Fourth, the strict inspection and verification regime ensures compliance. Lastly, while requiring all sides to live up to stringent requirements, the Treaty establishes a clear momentum that may have a positive affect on other areas of the developing European security architecture.

Implementation

Implementation of the CFE Treaty proceeded surprisingly well. The verification regime established targets for states to achieve during the 40 months outlined for implementation. This lengthy implementation period was deemed necessary because of the Treaty's overwhelming complexity and the monumental task of either removing or destroying a vast array of equipment – roughly 32,000 pieces of TLE for the Warsaw Pact and 16,000 for NATO. The Russian Federation alone was required to destroy over 10,000 pieces of TLE. By the initial target date of September 1993, each state had to have met 25% of its overall required reduction towards their respective allocation for each type of equipment. Further targets were established of 60% reduction by September 1994 and 100% reduction by 17 November 1995. Zone limitations were scheduled to become effective after the final reduction date in November 1995. The Treaty then specifies that four months be allocated to verify residual force levels. In May 1996, six months after final implementation and following the verification of residual levels, a Review Conference involving all signatories convened to discuss remaining difficulties, possible changes to the Treaty, and potential future agreements.

It is perhaps axiomatic for successful arms-control agreements that they receive their most intense public scrutiny during the initial negotiations, while little attention is paid to the actual implementation process. This was true for CFE until November 1995, when resolution of the flank issue came to the fore. All participants, except for Armenia and Azerbaijan because of their continuing conflict in Nagorno-Karabakh, reached their 25% and 60% reduction goals in September 1993 and 1994. Belarus had difficulty meeting the final deadline for reductions because of serious economic difficulties and the JCG agreed to extend the timetable for its final compliance until April 1996. Germany and the United States undertook to provide Belarus with material assistance to complete the destruction process.[3]

None of the inspections during the reduction period revealed discrepancies of any significance to suggest circumvention or violation of Treaty provisions. This was partly because the implementation process evolved to meet the changing political conditions in Europe. The preamble to the CFE Treaty includes a clause committing the signatories to strive 'to replace military confrontation with a new pattern of security relations based on peaceful cooperation'.[4] Although very specific in its technical content, the agreement does not indicate how these 'new patterns' are to be achieved. The North Atlantic Cooperation Council (NACC) – which includes all former members of the Warsaw Pact as well as NATO – was created in 1991 partly to readjust the security environment following the disintegration of the WTO. The NACC increased the flow of information and ideas about the implementation process. NATO ran seminars on verification for NACC members, Eastern European officers attended the NATO arms-control inspection course, and many capitals in the former Warsaw Pact acquired on-line access to NATO's verification data base, VERITY.

These new contacts have been formalised as NATO's Enhanced Cooperation Program. Among its activities, joint NATO-led multi-national inspections have been held including 'Cooperation Partners' from Central and Eastern Europe.[5] NATO's Partnership for Peace (PFP) may further expand these steps to permit non-NATO observers to participate in Western inspections. It may also allow non-signatories to the CFE Treaty, such as Slovenia, who have joined PFP to participate.

Continuing political change did, however, present NATO with problems as well as opportunities. Former Warsaw Pact members began to request CFE inspections of their former allies to ensure compliance with Treaty reductions. These so-called 'East-on-East' inspections illustrate the emerging security concerns of Central European countries, but, since the total number of inspections per year for any one state is limited, they also reduced the total number of inspections available to NATO of those East European states of particular interest, such as the Russian Federation and Ukraine.

The Problem of the Flanks
Despite the optimism generated by the steady progress of imple-mentation, serious difficulties arose that ultimately resulted in the Russian Federation being in violation of the CFE Treaty at final implementation on 17 November 1995. The problem concerns the restrictions, listed in Article V of the CFE Treaty, placed on Russian and Ukrainian forces in the so-called 'flank' zone, and could ultimately imperil the whole accord. Russian officials have steadfastly argued since 1993 for Article V to be removed from the CFE Treaty.

For NATO, the flank zone includes Turkey, Greece and Norway. For the former Warsaw Pact and CIS, this area includes all of Romania, Bulgaria, Moldova, Armenia, Georgia, Azerbaijan and a portion of both Russia and Ukraine, as amended by the 1992 Tashkent Agreement. This latter portion consists of the North Caucasus and Leningrad Military Districts in the Russian Federation plus the south-eastern third of Ukraine (a portion of the Odessa Military District). The total amount of equipment Russian forces in active units are allowed in this area is 700 tanks, 1,280 artillery pieces and 580 ACVs out of the Russian Federation's total CFE allocation. Article V further allows Russia to place 600 tanks, 400 artillery pieces and 800 ACVs in designated permanent storage sites in the northern portion of the flank (i.e., the Leningrad Military District). The idea of a separate 'flank zone' was the result of efforts by Turkey and Norway, neither of which wanted Soviet forces removed from the central region to reappear on their borders.

US officials first became aware of Russian concerns about the flank limits in early 1993.[6] Russian Defence Minister General Pavel Grachev, returning from an inspection tour of military units in the Transcaucasus, stated that the 'geopolitical situation has changed' since the Treaty had entered into force and that Russia 'now finds it necessary to reconsider the armed quotas envisioned by the [CFE] accords'. Later that same year, Grachev's press office reported that a Defence Ministry Collegium review of CFE quotas had 'expressed concern' that Treaty limitations were forcing Russia to distribute arms in the European part of the country 'without taking account of security interests'.[7]

Curiously, the problem of the flanks was formally presented to the JCG by Ukrainian Ambassador to the JCG Yuri Kostenko on 14 September 1993. Ambassador Kostenko pointed out that the flank limits placed on Ukraine were 'completely unjustified at the present time'. He further noted that the limits would force Ukraine to defend one-quarter of its territory with only 17% of its available tanks, 7% of its ACVs and 22% of its artillery.[8] This was quickly followed by a letter from Russian President Boris Yeltsin to all NATO leaders requesting that Article V of the CFE Treaty be eliminated. Yeltsin argued that the drastic changes in the political situation on the European continent and increased turmoil along Russia's border had invalidated these restrictions. Yeltsin also observed that the two Military Districts affected by Article V (Leningrad and North Caucasus) comprised over half the territory of European Russia, and the restraints were discriminatory since they were not imposed in a similar fashion on any Western state. The President declared that this problem needed to be solved quickly so that Russia could redeploy its forces properly and construct sufficient infrastructure to support them.[9]

The rationale presented by the Russians in the JCG and elsewhere remained consistent after autumn 1993 and revolved around their perception of Russia's national security interests. The Russian leadership presented seven arguments in its analysis:

- First, the drastically changed global political environment made the bloc-to-bloc basis of the Treaty invalid. In this regard, the Treaty unfairly discriminated against Russia by placing internal restrictions on where its forces could be positioned on its own territory.

- Second, the new Russian military doctrine that had received official governmental and parliamentary approval in late 1993 required a more balanced military defence.[10]

- Third, the logic of the flanks changed. Whereas in the days of the Soviet Union, the North Caucasus Military District was considered a rear area, it was now a border district.[11] Consequently, it was illogical to expect that deploying just 15% of Russian forces would be adequate to defend over half of European Russia.

- Fourth, the rising threat to stability, particularly from Muslim fundamentalism in the south, was the greatest challenge to Russian security and required a significant deployment of Russian forces to the North Caucasus.

- Fifth, the North Caucasus was more suitable for stationing forces returning to Russia because of its climate, as well as for economic and social reasons. In particular, the Russians argued, the region already had the necessary infrastructure in place to cope with returning forces.

- Sixth, changes to the Treaty would not set a precedent as it had evolved since it was first ratified. Russian spokesmen cited the example of the Baltic states, which had left the Treaty on gaining their independence, as well as the addition of the former members of the Soviet Union, the Czech Republic and Slovakia.[12]

- Finally, Russian spokesmen privately suggested that while the Russian government strongly supported the Treaty, it had caused serious disagreements between civil and military leaders both in Russia and earlier in the Soviet Union, and was not well regarded by many members of the military.[13] Russians leaders stressed that they were not seeking to discard the key elements of the Treaty, such as the reductions and associated inspections. They sought no increase in their total allocation of TLE under the CFE accord, but simply the removal of the Article V restrictions on where they could deploy their forces.

Russian experts have suggested several solutions to this problem. Initially, proposals focused exclusively on suspending Article V altogether. Later, they suggested that a large part of the North Caucasus be removed from the flanks and re-categorised as a 'rear district'. This proposal was coupled with vague assurances about the level of forces in the Leningrad Military District, no 'over concentration of forces' in the North Caucasus, and no abuse of Russia's right under CFE to station large quantities of equipment in Kaliningrad. The Russians also gave assurances that implementing these changes would not 'prejudice the security of any State Party to the Treaty'.[14]

In February 1994, the Russian Federation proposed new ideas. These attempted to avoid any suggestion of a 'change' in the Treaty, but rather a 'reinterpretation' of key aspects of it. One idea was exempting naval infantry and coastal defence forces from flank limits since including TLE associated with these forces had been a Soviet, not a Russian Federation, request. Some Russian officials also argued that this should be considered as an addition to the Treaty, but not as an integral part of the text. They further suggested that the authorisation to remove equipment from designated storage (allowed in the Treaty as a total for each 'group of states') be reinterpreted to mean that 'each state party' had this allowance. This would be coupled with the right to 'temporary deployments'.[15] Russian spokesmen also suggested that the 42 days for returning TLE to storage sites established in Article X be considered a 'recommendation' only.[16]

While the specific solution changed over time, Russian arguments and objectives remained consistent. The authorities sought to increase TLE in active forces (particularly those stationed in the North Caucasus region). They also wished to establish that the internal limitations imposed on Russia by the flank requirements were no longer valid and were inconsistent with Russian security.

Western negotiators opposed these solutions, and steadfastly argued that the Russian Federation must comply with the flank limitations, while also suggesting that the West would consider making adjustments at the May 1996 Review Conference. Officials of the NATO member-states initially feared that a change to the

Treaty, such as altering the map, would be considered so significant in their respective capitals that it would necessitate a second ratification vote – something all governments wished to avoid. Many also feared that any alteration to the Treaty prior to final implementation in November 1995 would provoke a flurry of additional proposed changes from other states that could jeopardise the entire accord. Western experts had discovered that, in the new security environment, achieving consensus on a NATO position was becoming increasingly difficult. At the same time, the nature of the process required a bilateral negotiation between the United States and Russia to be avoided at all cost.

Flank Limits and Ukraine
As noted above, the flank limits also restrict the deployment of forces within Ukraine's borders, which complicated reaching a solution satisfactory to all parties. Ukraine was adamant from September 1993 that the flank limitations be reviewed – for many of the same reasons cited by the Russian Federation. Ukrainian officials observed, for example, that the flank limits only allowed them a small percentage of their total TLE allocation in the southern portion of the Odessa Military District that is nearly one-quarter of their entire territory.[17]

Ukrainian defence experts also argued that their country required a more balanced distribution of its forces. Implementing the flank limitations would force them to position most of their troops in the north-western portion of the country (the Carpathian Military District). This deployment, they observed, would contravene the stated NATO goal of reducing forward deployed forces and the associated threat of surprise attack.[18] The issue was further exacerbated by the dissolution of the Soviet Union and emerging problems between Russia and Ukraine. These included the disappearance of the Kiev Military District which Ukraine had previously shared with Russia, and the division of Ukraine into only two districts – Carpathian and Odessa; the presence of Russian forces in eastern Moldova; and emerging Russian nationalism in the Crimea. In addition, the Russian Federation and Ukraine continued to negotiate the final distribution of TLE assigned to the naval infantry and coastal defence forces of the Black Sea Fleet. This issue had still not been resolved in April 1996 when President Yeltsin cancelled a scheduled visit to Kiev to sign a final agreement. However, most observers believe that cancelling the trip was motivated above all by domestic politics, specifically the Russian presidential elections scheduled for June.[19]

It was clear from the outset, however, that from the Ukrainian perspective the flank question was an issue of sovereignty. Ukrainian leaders wanted to establish their country as a mid-level power and not the spin-off of an old empire. With no solution to their own flank problems the Ukrainians were wary of the Russian Federation receiving any relief on the flanks that could pose additional threats to their own security. Implementing the flank limits also presented the Ukrainians with a serious economic problem. It required abandoning infrastructure in the restricted area and constructing new facilities in the Carpathian Military District and Northern Odessa, which Ukrainian officials deemed economically impossible.[20]

In spring 1995, Ukrainian negotiators declared that they could not achieve their flank limits because of the impasse in negotiations with Russia over ownership of TLE assigned to the Black Sea Fleet. They also noted that any forces in the flank area above their authorisation for that region were on a 'temporary deployment' of up to one year.[21] This use of Treaty 'flexibility' to solve Kiev's problem was, surprisingly, accepted by the other members of the JCG with little protest. It did not, however, permanently solve the Ukrainian problem, but pushed the search for an ultimate solution into the May 1996 Review Conference.

NATO's Position
While there is no doubt that the impasse over the flank zones threatens full implementation of the CFE Treaty – and perhaps its very existence – there were certain positive aspects to the manner in which the problem unfolded. All efforts by the parties involved were overt and there has been no attempt to disguise or hide the problem and the difficulties associated with it. Even constructing infrastructure for forces in the flank was reported publicly. All parties used the Joint Consultative Group to air the issues, illustrating that the procedures established in the Treaty were working – although whether the JCG was, in the final analysis, adequate to resolve this conflict is questionable. Lastly, the Russian military was extremely candid on the issue during all high-level military-to-military contacts throughout the three-year implementation period.

The public response of NATO members to the flank issue continuously emphasised the value of the CFE Treaty as the 'cornerstone of European security'. Officials argued that it could not be renegotiated, and to do so would establish a bad precedent for other arms-control forums. They included in this argument not only the basic text of the Treaty, but also all related documents, protocols and declarations. Furthermore, Western officials observed that the Russian Federation freely accepted the Treaty as negotiated, including the agreements with the former members of the Warsaw Pact and declarations by the Soviet Union before its demise. Any alteration to these documents (such as those proposed) could not occur until the Review Conference. US and European negotiators also argued that Russia had not sufficiently explained its analysis of new threats to its frontiers that would justify removing or modifying the flank limits.

The West also believed that the CFE Treaty provided sufficient 'flexibility' to meet Russian needs. US and UK representatives suggested the following possibilities early in 1994:

- Russian troops in the North Caucasus could be 'light' forces with equipment not limited by the CFE Treaty (e.g., trucks, infantry weapons, low-calibre artillery, and certain tracked vehicles that are not part of the ACV category). Such a force, they argued, would be more appropriate to the terrain of the Caucasus, as well as to threats of internal instability.
- The Russians should recognise that there is no flank limitation for their aircraft (either fixed or rotary wing) which could be moved rapidly from zone to zone to meet any emerging threat.
- They could transfer additional ACVs and other tracked vehicles to their internal security forces, as allowed in Articles III and XII. Article XII, for example, allows up to 1,000 ACVs to be placed with internal security forces. Six hundred of these ACVs may be in the 'flank zone'. It does not, however, allow any transfer of tanks or artillery to internal security forces.
- Equipment for Russian units in the flank zone could be stored outside the area, but close enough for rapid deployment in time of crisis.
- Russia and Ukraine might also seek to renegotiate their allocation with the other former members of the Soviet Union (Armenia, Azerbaijan, Georgia, Ukraine and Moldova) or the Warsaw Pact (Bulgaria or Romania) with forces in the flank zone.[22]

Privately, many officials expressed the view that the Treaty's overall importance transcended the concerns about the flank limits. Consequently, some NATO members showed a willingness to compromise within the NATO High Level Task Force (HLTF), the body used by the Alliance to discuss its position on issues relating to the Treaty. Germany, for example, appeared sensitive to Russian concerns throughout the implementation period and co-sponsored proposals with Russia for less costly destruction procedures. The Germans also suggested that the timetable for destroying equipment might be extended, or that excess equipment not destroyed at the end of the reduction period could be placed temporarily at secure storage sites pending final destruction.[23]

Other NATO countries were less sympathetic to Russian proposals throughout the implementation process. France, for example, uniformly opposed any concession to the Russian Federation. French officials feared that any change to the Treaty would result in multiple proposals by other signatories to alter parts of the Treaty they objected to, thereby threatening the entire basis of the accord. Turkey and Norway were the most outspoken against any compromise because they border the flank areas.[24] They argued that increasing the numbers of Russian forces in the flank zone would reduce warning time and be counter to their security interests, and that changing the Treaty flank limits could kill CFE altogether, opening the way for a new European arms race.

As the process moved into spring 1995, it became clear that Turkey was in many ways the principal opponent of any concession to the Russian Federation. Turkish opposition may, however, have been more politically than militarily motivated. While increased Russian forces in the flank are a concern, they do not suggest an imminent threat, and Turkey still enjoys NATO security guarantees. Turkish officials have become increasingly concerned, however, about perceived Russian imperialist ambitions in the Caucasus. This concern was strengthened by the Russian invasion of Chechnya in December 1994. Many Turkish leaders also believe that Russia is the primary impetus behind the hostilities in Georgia, as well as the war between Armenia and Azerbaijan over Nagorno-Karabakh. They argue that increased Russian force levels in the flank area indicate Moscow's desire to reassert a degree of control over the former Soviet republics of Georgia, Armenia, Azerbaijan and Moldova. These developments clearly conflict with long-term Turkish foreign-policy objectives in the region. As a result, Turkey has hinted that any concessions on the flank issue could result in it reviewing its continued participation in the accord. Given the strong feelings on the issue in Turkey – and, to a lesser degree, Norway – NATO's efforts to establish a formal alliance approach to solving the problem were deadlocked for nearly 18 months.

The View from Moscow

There can be no doubt that the flank issue was a surrogate for broader internal and external problems facing the Russian Federation. It illustrates, for example, the continuing friction between several players in Russia's bureaucratic and civil–military circles. The Russian military was sceptical of the CFE Treaty from the outset and questioned whether it had adequate resources following its full implementation to defend the political and territorial integrity of the country.[25] But the military is far from a unitary actor. The appointment in 1992 of General Pavel Grachev as Russia's first Minister of Defence caused resentment among senior officers on the General Staff that still continues. It is likely that many senior Russian officers blame him, at least partially, for Russia's continued implementation of the Treaty despite his repeated criticisms of CFE.[26] Grachev has also had serious disagreements with General Anatoly Kulikov, head of the Internal Security Forces, and General Andrei Nikolayev, Commander of the Border Troops, over resources, the potential transfer of army assets to these respective forces, and major military exercises.[27] As a result, the Russian Ministry of Defence has continually rejected transferring ACVs to the Internal Security Forces as a partial solution to the flank impasse. There have also been differences between the military, Foreign Ministry and the Office of the President over issues such as Russian participation in NATO's Partnership for Peace.[28] These tensions led to suggestions that the civil authorities were losing control of the military.[29] Civilians may be unable to force the Russian armed forces to compromise, even if they wanted to do so.

If there was ever a chance of finding a solution to the flank problem prior to the November 1995 deadline, it may have ended with Russia's invasion of Chechnya in the southern portion of the flank zone. Following the Chechens' stiff resistance, President Yeltsin announced the formation of the 58th Army in Grozny in June 1995. This announcement was followed by the suggestion that an 'exclusion zone' should be created to encompass all Russian forces deployed to Chechnya. Such a zone would remove all forces inside its boundaries from the CFE total and would exclude 2,850 items of TLE from the flank limit. Western acceptance of this idea would have eliminated the need for any additional withdrawal of Russian forces from the flank area.[30] This proposal was doomed from the start, but Russian negotiators continued to repeat it with regularity throughout most of 1995.

As the Chechen war has continued it has become evident that Defence Ministry 'hardliners', led by General Grachev, have played an increasingly important role in CFE and other issues, to the overall detriment of Russian civil–military relations. Developments in early 1996 suggest that the chances of a negotiated settlement of the Chechen conflict are receding, and Moscow may have decided that force is the only option. Furthermore, the sorry state of the Russian Army, revealed by its disastrous operational performance in Chechnya, makes it less likely that military leaders in Moscow will entertain a compromise over CFE. If Russia eventually succeeds in subduing the Chechens, there can be little doubt that it will wish to maintain a large occupation force in the region. Either of these possibilities make it unlikely that the Russian Federation will accept the flank limits without alteration.

Russian critics of the CFE Treaty, while describing the 'flank issue' as discriminatory, have repeatedly pointed out how the Treaty places the Russian Federation in an inferior position. As the November 1995 deadline for implementation arrived, General Grachev commented: 'We are not now prepared to respect the current treaty on conventional arms reduction in Europe. The treaty in its present form completely excludes minimal security measures for our state.'[31] Many Russians argue that the CFE Treaty is a concerted effort by the West to 'keep Russia down' and shows a lack of willingness by the United States to develop a true 'strategic partnership' with Russia.[32] This opinion is widely held by the Russian military, but several political parties during the 1993 presidential and 1995 parliamentary elections claimed that Russia's compliance with CFE and the Strategic Arms Reduction Talks (START II) Treaty was contrary to Russian national security. It also appears to continue to be 'good politics' to oppose concessions on the CFE flank issue as Russian politicians prepare for the presidential election in June 1996.

Resolution of this problem is tied not only to Russia's domestic politics and relations with the West, but also to its future relations with the former members of the Soviet Union and perceived responsibilities towards the so-called 'near abroad' (Russian citizens living outside the borders of the Federation). Added to these perceptions is the widespread view that Russia faces future external threats and continuing strife on its borders, particularly in the Caucasus. Russia's new military doctrine suggests that restoring and expanding a mutually advantageous relationship between Russia and the other members of the CIS must be a priority. Russian officials start from the premise that their country's security is indivisible from the security of the other Commonwealth states.[33] In other words, Moscow considers its forward defence to begin at the borders of the former Soviet Union and not the Russian Federation. Consequently, Russian military planners believe that they must position forces on the territory of these states – Armenia, Moldova, Georgia and Azerbaijan – and along Russia's borders with them.

The deployment of Russian forces on the territory of the North Caucasian republics began in summer 1994 when Russian troops moved to the Georgian–Abkhazian border ostensibly to assist in settling the Georgian civil war.[34] The Status of Forces agreement signed in 1995 by Russia and Georgia states the level of Russian military presence and activity permitted on Georgian territory. It allows basing facilities for two Russian divisions, the presence of Russian border guards on the Georgian–Turkish border, the use of Georgian airspace by Russian military aircraft, access to all telecommunications facilities, use of all training facilities, and a lease to Georgia's Poti naval base for the Russian Black Sea Fleet. By summer 1995, Russian forces in Georgia were slightly under two motorised rifle divisions. Georgia also agreed to transfer its unused TLE allocations of 115 tanks, 160 ACVs and 170 artillery pieces to Russia. Moscow had a similar arrangement with Armenia. Russian troop strength in Armenia is roughly 9,000 (approximately one motorised rifle division), and the Armenian government agreed to reduce its TLE ceilings by 80 tanks, 160 ACVs and 85 artillery pieces. This equipment would then be transferred to the Russian allocation for the flank. Moldova also has on its territory the Russian 14th Army (roughly 6,400 troops) undertaking peacekeeping missions, but no agreement to transfer any portion of Moldovan TLE to Moscow has been made public.[35] Any transfer of TLE allocations, however, will have to be accepted by all signatories to the 1992 Tashkent Agreement, which initially divided the allocation of the Soviet Union and is still valid under international law.

Russia has also pressured Azerbaijan to accept a sizeable Russian 'peacekeeping' force on its territory. Moscow has shown continued interest in Azerbaijan, largely because of its vast oil reserves and plans to construct an export pipeline. Azerbaijani leaders have resisted Russian overtures and requests that they cede a portion of their TLE to Moscow.[36] They have also continuously proclaimed the inadmissibility of stationing Russian forces on Azerbaijan's territory and have demanded in the JCG that CFE inspections be made of Russian Federation forces in Armenia. Azerbaijan's Deputy Foreign Minister Araz Azimov stated that if Russia raises the issue of the flank zone, then the question of its forces stationed in Armenia must also be considered.[37] In fact, the Azerbaijan delegation to the JCG temporarily blocked the adoption of a statement by the 30 signatories that described excess Russian forces in the flank area as 'technical non-compliance' at the Treaty deadline in November 1995. The Azeris did this to underscore their opposition to Armenia allowing the temporary deployment of Russian forces on Armenian territory without careful scrutiny by the West.[38]

NATO's Compromise Proposal

In an effort to bridge this gap before the official 17 November 1995 deadline for CFE Treaty implementation, the United States put forward a compromise solution to the flank impasse. This was accepted by all NATO members and officially presented to the Russian Federation in September 1995. The plan envisaged redrawing the map that describes the military districts in the flank area. The proposal would remove five *oblasts* from the flank, three in the north and two in the south. This 'shrinking' of the flank zone would meet most of Russia's demands for increases in tanks and artillery, but it would still need to remove or destroy approximately 1,700 ACVs in the flank area. Russia would also be required to grant additional inspections in flank and 'former' flank areas, expand the number of information exchanges, and place unspecified limits on equipment in certain 'former' flank areas.[39] The proposal would also remove one *oblast* from the Ukrainian portion of the flank – which would solve Kiev's problem as well.

Even after receiving NATO's compromise proposal, Russian officials remained sceptical. Colonel General Aleksandr Galkin, Chief of the Main Directorate for Armoured Troops in the Russian Ministry of Defence, commented in an interview in early November 1995 that, 'to date for the Russian war department there has been no nastier strangulation of Russia's defence interests than the agreement of the then leadership of the USSR [Mikhail Gorbachev] to the conditions of the flank limitations'. General Galkin did, however, reiterate Russia's commitment to meet its overall national totals.[40] Some Russian officials totally dismissed NATO's proposal to redraw the map as 'a propaganda move rather than a real step toward a solution to the problem'.[41] Many Russian parliamentarians in the Duma were also sceptical of the proposed plan.[42]

As the 17 November 1995 deadline arrived, the JCG agreed on a communiqué on the same day that, as mentioned above, described the Russian position as 'technical non-compliance'. It further declared that all states had shown a willingness to find a solution to the impasse and that a process was in place to move in that direction. The official Russian position described the West's proposal as a major concession and a framework for further discussions. Russian negotiators also suggested further alterations to the proposed 'new' map and stated their opposition to the additional implementing measures designed to expand transparency over the region.[43]

While the Turkish delegation to the JCG accepted this communiqué, the reaction in Ankara was far from supportive. Then Prime Minister Tansu Ciller stressed that Turkey was unwilling to make further concessions to Moscow. The official spokesman for the Turkish Foreign Ministry emphasised that CFE was an issue between Russia and NATO, and not Turkey. A leading Turkish newspaper summarised Ankara's perspective as follows:

> The real issue is the struggle over spheres of influence in the Caucasus. With the military power that it wants to retain Russia not only plans to crush the independence movement in Chechnya, but also to reduce Turkey's influence in the Caucasus. One cannot take up the flank issue as separate from regional oil pipelines, military coups, civil wars, and bomb attacks. The thing which should disturb us is not our Western friends' acceptance of Russian demands to retain military power in the flanks, but their silence to the attitude which views the southern Caucasus as Russia's backyard.[44]

Throughout spring 1996, the NATO countries – led by the United States – continued to search for a compromise that would satisfy both Russia and Turkey. This was complicated by the Turkish general elections in December 1995 that resulted in a long search for a viable coalition to establish a new government in Ankara. In Moscow, the Russian parliamentary elections, also in December 1995, which resulted in a major success for the Communist Party, signalled the beginning of the campaign leading up to the presidential elections scheduled for June 1996. This electoral activity, coupled with several serious military reversals in Chechnya, dimmed prospects for a settlement. Despite repeated efforts, no solution to the flank problem could be found prior to the May 1996 CFE Review Conference.

III. THE WAY AHEAD

The future of conventional arms control and its effect on European security depend on three factors. First, the CFE Treaty must be maintained, albeit in a modified form, as a basis for the region's security. This can only succeed if remaining difficulties, such as the flank issue, are resolved. Furthermore, the May 1996 Review Conference must, at a minimum, establish a *process* to consider other problem areas in the Treaty and its relationship to emerging security issues such as NATO enlargement. Second, conventional arms control must acquire a sub-regional focus if it is to adapt to the new security challenges in Europe and be consistent with the new NATO strategic concept. In this regard, a general framework approach is valuable, and the preliminary efforts by several countries to consider many aspects of the CFE Treaty and CSBMs in their sub-regional contexts are important. Finally, the arms-control portion of the November 1995 General Framework Agreement for Peace in Bosnia and Herzegovina must be negotiated and implemented to show how conventional arms control can be used as part of a peace agreement.

The CFE Review Conference
The CFE Treaty is designed to continue with no time limit, but it may need to be updated to conform to emerging realities. Article XXI of the Treaty requires the signatories to meet 46 months after entry into force and at five-year intervals thereafter to 'conduct a review of the operation of this Treaty'.[1] The initial May 1996 Review Conference is scheduled to last two weeks and its final report is likely to be presented at the OSCE meeting in Lisbon in early December.

Some Western states have argued that the Conference agenda should be limited to a simple examination of problems associated with the Treaty's implementation. These include the issue of the flank zone, questions raised by inspection teams during the implementation period, and additional confidence- and security-building measures. Supporters of this position are concerned that an unrestricted agenda would engender a plethora of proposed changes to the Treaty that could well undermine the progress already made in adopting it. While this argument has some merit, it will be extremely difficult, if not impossible, to sustain in a multilateral negotiation among sovereign states. Furthermore, the argument does not have the support of most NATO members. Instead, the

Conference could establish how the Treaty will serve the emerging European security architecture. It must institute a process that allows for Treaty 'modernisation' to be considered and discussed once the Conference ends. Failing to consider such modernisation would either allow the Treaty to drift into irrelevance, or result in an Extraordinary Conference, in accordance with Articles XX and XI, to consider formal requests for amendments. The following issues must be considered in the framework of the Review Conference.

Equipment East of the Urals
As described in Chapter II, one of the obstacles to final US Senate ratification of the CFE Treaty was the massive movement of Soviet equipment to the east of the Ural Mountains, outside the area of Treaty application. This took place immediately before the Treaty was signed and contributed significantly to the delay of roughly 18 months between signature and full ratification by the NATO states. The West's concerns led to a Soviet political commitment in June 1991, later accepted by Russia, to destroy or convert an additional 14,500 pieces of equipment (6,000 battle tanks, 7,000 artillery pieces and 1,500 ACVs). Although this commitment did not require the equipment to be destroyed by the very precise methods described in the CFE Treaty, it did require the Soviet Union, and subsequently the Russian Federation, to provide 'sufficient visible evidence' of their reduction. From the very beginning of the implementation period, however, serious concerns arose over the pace and validation of these reductions.

In early 1996, Russia confirmed that it had failed to meet the agreed 1 January 1996 deadline for destroying this equipment.[2] Even prior to this date, Russian spokesmen had complained about the excessive costs of destruction and delays in appropriating the necessary defence budget funds. Colonel General Galkin argued that the cost of destroying a single tank was 5.6 million roubles and that it cost 4.0m roubles to destroy an armoured vehicle. By April 1996, Russian officials had acknowledged the destruction of only about 30% of the total. Senior officials have contended that the money required to complete the destruction is not available. They also complain that only limited finances are available to procure new equipment, making it impossible to replenish the existing pool of equipment for active forces. Instead, many in the Russian Defence Ministry believe that it is no longer in their country's interest to scrap this equipment, arguing that even though outmoded, it should be retained in reserve.[3]

As a 'political' rather than 'legal' obligation of the Treaty, destroying this equipment could be raised in the US Senate or in the parliament of any other state which had supported the Treaty's ratification partly because the Soviet Union, and then Russia, had accepted this requirement. Furthermore, although much of the equipment is no longer militarily viable because of its long exposure to the elements, some may argue that Russia's stance on this question, coupled with other outstanding issues, suggest a pattern of non-compliance. The problem might be assuaged to some degree if Western inspectors had more immediate access to the area east of the Urals where the equipment is stored. Increased transparency on the condition and disposition of the TLE would verify whether or not it posed a militarily significant threat. The Russians could also allow continued surveillance while it rendered the equipment useless. But Russian officials have steadfastly refused additional access to this TLE, largely out of a fear that this would in essence expand the area of application beyond the Urals and hence beyond the Treaty definition.

One way to increase transparency and to demonstrate cooperation would be for Russia to identify the equipment's storage locations, to segregate it from active units, and for the Duma finally to ratify the Treaty on Open Skies. As well as increasing transparency significantly in this region, these measures would reassure Western security experts that this equipment posed no significant threat, and be consistent with the Treaty on Open Skies' aim of improving the monitoring of existing agreements.

Article V and the Flank Zone
Russia or Ukraine may continue to press for the removal of Article V as a solution to the problem of the flank zone. While some experts believe that incentives could have been offered prior to the Review Conference to keep the issue off the agenda, or at least limit discussion, several factors suggest otherwise. First, the Russian government has made a major issue of the flank question since President Yeltsin's initial letter to NATO leaders of September 1993. Ignoring the issue at the Review Conference would invite heavy criticism by Russian nationalists in the run-up the June presidential elections. Second, the flank question affects Ukraine as well as the Russian Federation. The solution adopted by the Ukrainian government to declare forces in excess to their entitlement on 'temporary deployment' was clearly a short-term expedient that will expire when the Conference convenes.

Russian officials will argue, as they have in the past, that the flank zone does not reflect current conditions and is discriminatory. Moscow will also continue negotiating with Moldova, Georgia and Armenia to obtain a portion of their respective entitlements and station Russian forces on their territory. The Russians are unlikely, however, to gain the level of forces they believe is necessary to maintain security, particularly in the North Caucasus following the invasion of Chechnya. Stationing significant additional forces outside the territory of the Russian Federation, but inside the current flank area, will also be difficult as long as Article V remains in its current form, since it places a limit of only 153 tanks, 241 ACVs and 140 artillery pieces for stationed forces in the flank zone.

Russian negotiators have attempted to strengthen their arguments for increasing their TLE at the 'expense' of the North Caucasian states and stationed forces by pressing for the exclusion of Federation forces involved in 'peacekeeping operations'. Personnel participating in such operations are exempt from limitations under CFE-1A, but this does not include TLE limited by CFE. Russian leaders have argued that the Russian Federation, working within the authority of the CIS, should have primary responsibility for peacekeeping operations within the borders of the former Soviet Union. Former Foreign Minister Andrei Kozyrev initially broached this issue in a speech given at the United Nations on 2 September 1993. Kozyrev sought recognition and financial support for Russian peacekeeping operations in the 'near abroad', arguing that Russia must either 'learn to conduct military actions to support and establish peace in the zones of our traditional geopolitical interests or we risk losing influence there and the vacuum will be filled by others'.[4] General Grachev also raised this issue in discussions with UN Secretary-General Boutros Boutros-Ghali in April 1994. Grachev asserted that if the conflict in Rwanda is settled by the Organisation of African Unity and operations in Haiti are conducted under the aegis of the Organisation of American States, why should operations by the CIS not be sanctioned under the UN Charter? Grachev further contended that forces assigned to peacekeeping operations and their authorised armaments should not count towards the maximum levels permissible under the CFE Treaty. Otherwise, the deployment of units trained for peacekeeping, such as the 45th Motorised Rifle Division based in the Leningrad Military District, could not be replaced while operating in Tajikistan or elsewhere in the CIS.[5]

This theme was reiterated when President Yeltsin addressed the United Nations prior to holding a summit with US President Bill

Clinton in autumn 1994. Yeltsin declared that Russia has similar rights to those of the United States in quelling disturbances on its borders. He added: 'The main peacekeeping burden in the territory of the former Soviet Union lies upon the Russian Federation'.[6] This was reiterated more formally a year later in Yeltsin's decree of 14 September 1995 on the 'Strategic Policy of the Russian Federation towards CIS Member States'.[7] More recently, the Russian President emphasised that Russia must invigorate a CIS integration process and retain vital interests in various 'spheres in the former USSR space'.[8]

Stationing Russian forces on the territory of other states in the North Caucasus has obvious implications for the flank problem. Russian thinking on peacekeeping is embedded in its September 1995 'Strategic Policy' and is quite different from Western views. The Russian military does not necessarily see 'normal' peace-keeping as low-intensity conflict that can be accomplished by light forces. Rather, it sees such operations as necessary to prevent a conflict escalating. Consequently, the Russians believe these opera-tions are appropriate for heavy forces. It is interesting that the Russian word *mirotvorets*, generally translated in English as 'peace*keeper*', literally means 'peace*maker*'. Russian peacekeeping experts often use their operations in Afghanistan as examples, and the General responsible for peacekeeping, Boris Pyankov, observed: 'Here in Russia, everything is the other way round ... first we use overwhelming force, then we bring the parties to the negotiating table'.[9] In a 21 June 1994 interview in *Krasnaya Zvezda*, Russian Deputy Defence Minister Colonel General Georgy Kondratev noted that the Ministry of Defence was preparing 2–3 motorised rifle divisions for peacekeeping (or peace-making) operations.[10]

In sum, Russian national policy, combined with the reluctance of other UN members to become involved in peacekeeping along the southern border of the Russian Federation, gives the Russian military an additional argument either for exceeding their flank authorisations, or for removing Article V entirely from the CFE Treaty. Equally, however, it will be extremely difficult (if not impossible) for any Western state to endorse Russian 'peace-keeping' operations along its borders. The deployment of Russian forces on the territory of states in the North Caucasus (Moldova, Georgia, Armenia and potentially Azerbaijan) and discussions on eliminating the flank limits have increased anxiety elsewhere in Eastern Europe. Latvian Chief of Staff Colonel Juris Arness, concerned about expanded Russian troop levels in the northern portion of the flank, observed: 'It is not a sign of independence to have their [i.e., Russian] forces in your country'.[11] This issue has also caused the Swedish Defence Ministry to revise its defence estimates in 1995, and Swedish Supreme Commander Owe Wiktorin expressed his disquiet at the possibility of a dramatic increase in Russian forces around St Petersburg.[12]

Extending the Treaty

Outside the Russian Federation there is little interest in extending the CFE Treaty to include other pieces of equipment or negotiating lower levels of TLE for the participating states. Although many countries have chosen to deploy forces smaller than their respective entitlement, none seems interested in seeing its allocation reduced further, since they wish to maintain a hedge against future security difficulties. Some Russian security experts have proposed initiating discussions on further reductions and even expanding the categories of equipment involved.[13] These proposals have included adding naval forces to the arms-reduction process and placing limits on naval activities.[14] Such suggestions are normally couched in a desire to see the OSCE assume a greater role, the creation of new zones, the elimination of bloc ceilings, and the development of new sub-regional arrangements. It is difficult to separate additional reductions from these other proposals as well as to assess the degree to which such recommendations are genuine.

Destruction Procedures

Many parties agree that TLE destruction procedures and costs must be reviewed and several states have openly complained that the precise procedures made implementation very expensive. Belarus declared in spring 1995 that it could no longer continue to destroy equipment because it lacked the necessary funds and is willing for NATO inspectors to examine the equipment it has segregated for destruction. Indeed, this equipment is often so degraded by exposure to weather and lack of maintenance that it is clearly militarily ineffective. Still, some experts are concerned that Belarus' failure to comply may have been encouraged by Moscow, as Russia did not wish to be the only state in non-compliance in November 1995.

The CFE Treaty is silent on the procedures states parties must use to maintain numerical limitations once residual equipment levels have been verified. Some participants have already questioned whether destroying TLE to authorised levels, and then maintaining these levels, must follow the strict guidelines established in the

Treaty. There are two possible solutions. First, the West could insist on adhering to the procedures required to maintain each state's authorised totals. This approach has little or no support among NATO or the other Treaty signatories. Second, equipment that is retired or replaced could be destroyed by any means, including environmental exposure, in order to maintain national limits.

The West pushed for such stringent procedures from the start out of a concern that the vast quantities of equipment the Warsaw Pact would have to destroy to reach its required limits might instead be exported to another part of the world, thus contributing to global instability. Hence the view developed that transparency must be maintained on equipment removed from service. [15]

However, exporting significant quantities of TLE as a result of force modernisation is unlikely in the near future. Given budgetary constraints, it is difficult to imagine that any individual state will modernise its forces to such a degree that it would be left with significant military hardware to export. Other agreements are also in place to help to restrain the indiscriminate export of conventional military equipment, particularly to 'rogue' states. For example, the UN Register of Conventional Arms, established on 1 January 1992, uses concepts and categories developed for CFE, and increases transparency on imports and exports of arms. Although not a panacea, it has achieved modest success. [16]

On 19 December 1995, 28 countries agreed to the Wassenaar Arrangement establishing export controls on conventional weaponry and dual-use technologies. Once again, the states involved adopted the categories of equipment described in the CFE Treaty and UN Register. The Arrangement calls on states to provide information twice a year to the other signatories, with additional details, such as the models and types of weapons exported. [17] This arrangement, however, is not a perfect solution to the problem of potential large-scale arms transfers to areas of instability. It does not, for example, include all of the former states of the Warsaw Pact (Belarus, Bulgaria, Ukraine and Romania have not participated) and only provides for notification 'after the fact'. Although a dispute between Russia and the United States over a critical provision has placed the agreement on hold, the Wassenaar Arrangement does illustrate a degree of cooperation between NATO countries and the Russian Federation on this issue. [18]

Experts remain optimistic that these difficulties can be reconciled, and that the Wassenaar Arrangement might be used as a criterion for NATO membership. Finally, while the CFE Treaty may never be extended to include other categories of equipment, the procedures established in the Treaty to update the Protocol on Existing Types of Conventional Armaments and Equipment (POET) limited by CFE must be strictly followed in order to categorise new TLE models as they come into service.

Bloc-to-Bloc Limits
Several East European states are likely to propose that the 'bloc-to-bloc' character of the CFE Treaty be removed since one of the original groups of states parties – the Warsaw Pact – no longer exists. Although this may be inevitable, its implications must be thoroughly considered. For example, this change would have a significant effect on the verification regime and the way in which inspections are allocated and conducted. More importantly, NATO would lose the flexibility to shift forces or entitlements between its members. NATO exercised this option during the implementation period, transferring more up-to-date equipment (most notably M60 tanks) to allies in the southern tier who were destroying older equipment, a procedure known as 'cascading'. As a result, some states now have more modern forces after implementation than they did prior to November 1990. Turkey, for example, has actually acquired more equipment since implementation – due to a NATO decision on respective entitlements for its membership consistent with the overall ceiling – and has also greatly modernised its forces. Although it did not expand its forces in all categories to its authorised ceiling, it did make significant increases. The following are equipment holdings for Turkey at the Treaty's entry into force in 1992 and its final authorised ceilings for November 1995:[19]

	entry into force (1992)	ceiling (1995)
tanks	2,823	2,795
ACVs	1,502	3,120
artillery	3,442	3,523
helicopters	5	103
aircraft	511	750

Note: These totals, however, do not include forces located in south-eastern Turkey not limited by the Treaty.

While one of the purposes of the CFE Treaty was to reduce the East–West force imbalance, particularly in Central Europe, some experts suggest that cascading equipment, coupled with the dissolution of the Warsaw Pact, has shifted the imbalance elsewhere. Some believe that this is a strong argument for abandoning group limits. Bulgarian officials, for example, have voiced deep concern about NATO transferring equipment to its southern members.[20] Both Greece and Turkey received greater entitlements within the Alliance as they began to modernise their forces and both benefited from cascading. By contrast, Bulgaria's forces are in poor condition and no longer 'enjoy' the security benefits of Warsaw Pact membership. Furthermore, Bulgarian defence budgets have hardly been able to sustain the daily living needs of its army, let alone pay for equipment modernisation. As a partial response, Russia announced in June 1995 the transfer of 100 T72 tanks, 100 BMP armoured infantry fighting vehicles, and 24 Mi-24 helicopters to Bulgaria under a cascading programme similar to that of NATO.[21]

Some experts suggest that eliminating the bloc-to-bloc approach would force the 'sufficiency rule' to be reconsidered. The sufficiency rule introduces at least the concept of national limits into the CFE Treaty by restricting the holdings of any single party. It was originally set at about 30% of theatre totals, and no individual state could exceed the following limits:

Tanks	Artillery	ACVs	Helicopters	Aircraft
13,300	13,700	20,000	1,500	5,150

This was judged to be the greatest acceptable constraint on Soviet forces, and would have required the Soviet Union to make significant reductions. Soviet acceptance of this limit satisfied the original aim of the sufficiency rule, and the subsequent demise of both the Warsaw Pact and the Soviet Union further removed the concern that any individual state could amass preponderant forces on the European continent. Although the force level established in the CFE Treaty is quite high, the sufficiency rule still illustrates that all state parties accept this important principle. Consequently, while efforts to negotiate a lower sufficiency rule might have some merit, it may be difficult to find a new level satisfactory to all parties. This would also focus attention away from more relevant issues.

Revamping the CFE Treaty sub-zones may be necessary to maintain stability among national totals. This could be done by introducing three general zones: central, northern and southern. In each case, traditional antagonists would be placed in the same sub-zone, which would include both NATO and non-NATO states. The northern zone, for example, might include Kaliningrad, Poland, Norway, Denmark and the Leningrad Military District of the Russian Federation (generally a Baltic area). A sub-zonal ceiling would be established for each category of equipment, which would be the sum of the countries' current entitlements instead of separate equipment ceilings for each group. As a result, any increase in an individual state's TLE entitlements would have to be acceptable to all other states in that sub-zone and within the overall ceiling. This change might reduce some of the security concerns of states like Bulgaria and would be another way to ease the process of NATO enlargement.

CFE and NATO Enlargement
Adjustments to the CFE Treaty and conventional arms control in general could play an important role in NATO enlargement. NATO clearly hopes that the cooperative climate established by CFE, together with the creation of the NACC and PFP, will help to reduce national suspicions and foster the confidence necessary to admit former Warsaw Pact members into NATO without isolating the Russian Federation. The September 1995 'NATO Study on Enlargement' acknowledges the '[CFE] Treaty's continued fundamental role in building and maintaining European security', and stresses that the 'NATO Allies consider the CFE Treaty as the cornerstone of European security'.[22] The study does not, however, describe the implications of NATO enlargement for the Treaty, but defers that analysis until enlargement actually takes place.[23] Although this position was appropriate for the NATO study, it will hardly suffice for much longer.

Moscow is totally opposed to NATO enlargement, and its opposition has been both unified and vitriolic.[24] Western supporters of NATO enlargement have argued that the Alliance has always been defensive and that its enlargement will 'stabilise' Eastern Europe, enhancing rather than degrading Russian security. From Moscow's perspective, enlargement is part of an overall effort to deny Russia an appropriate role in developing a new European security arrangement. The key political problem is that Moscow views NATO enlargement as an effort to isolate rather than to integrate the Russian Federation into a new security architecture. This level of insecurity has been exacerbated by the dismal performance of the Russian Army in Chechnya. Alexei Arbatov, a member of the Duma and leading security expert, characterised the Russian Army in

Chechnya as 'severely disorganised, weakened and mismanaged. It is probably at the lowest point since June 1941, when it suffered a catastrophic initial defeat at the hands of the German Wehrmacht'.[25]

Russian officials have threatened that NATO enlargement would have severe consequences for East–West relations. Minister of Defence Grachev suggested in meetings with US Secretary of Defense William Perry and Ukrainian Defence Minister Valery Shmarov that enlargement would force Moscow to review its adherence to CFE and the role of tactical nuclear weapons in Russian defence planning.[26] This latter threat was underscored in an article in *Pravda* in October 1995 which reported that the Russian General Staff had prepared a new draft military doctrine in response to the perceived threat of NATO enlargement. This new doctrine proposed deploying tactical nuclear weapons to western Russia, Belarus, Kaliningrad and aboard Russian warships of the Baltic Fleet. The draft doctrine also recommended that Russia should occupy the Baltic states – Estonia, Latvia and Lithuania – if NATO extends them membership.[27] Other officials have stated that enlargement would 'blow up' the CFE Treaty and adversely affect the evolution of democracy in the Russian Federation.[28] A paper entitled 'Russia and NATO' prepared by the Russian Council on Foreign and Defence Policy in June 1995 and signed by over 50 members of the Duma and leading security experts, echoed these views, and further stated that NATO enlargement would encourage Russia to seek allies to its south and east, enhance efforts to transform the CIS into a defence system, and severely undermine those seeking better relations with the West.[29]

Some advocates have suggested that in legal terms NATO can enlarge without any changes being made to the CFE Treaty, because the Treaty is not between two alliances, but between states. According to this view, individual states are signatories to the Treaty and therefore may change their alliance status without upsetting the Treaty system. While this interpretation might be correct in a strictly legal sense, it would seem to contradict Article II of the Treaty which clearly defines the term 'group of States Parties' as referring to the signatories to the Treaty of Warsaw (1955) and the Treaty of Washington (1948) respectively, and even lists the alliance status of each state separately. This definition, coupled with Articles IV and VII, fixes very definitively and legally the associated overall limits for each bloc and in each respective sub-zone (see Chapter I, Table 2). Any effort to ignore this portion of the agreement might encourage those countries, especially Russia, that are seeking to abandon the bloc-to-bloc character of the CFE Treaty, at the same time calling into question the good intentions of the West.

In technical terms, maintaining an alliance total for TLE might be useful for restraining NATO within those ceilings, even if it acquires new members. For example, if the Visegrad states – Hungary, Poland, Slovakia and the Czech Republic – were admitted to NATO, the alliance would still have to adhere to the overall limits (i.e., 20,000 tanks) and would consequently have to adjust the allowed totals for its other members accordingly. Furthermore, some adjustment might be required in the respective portion of each state's entitlement in active forces since NATO, for example, is only authorised 16,500 tanks in active units in the entire Atlantic to the Urals region. Conversely, the amount of TLE allocated to the Visegrad states as a result of the 1991 Warsaw Pact negotiations in Budapest could be subdivided among its remaining former members.

This proposal has a certain mathematical attraction, and would also appear to parallel the continuing Western interest in reducing the level of preponderant power in Central Europe. But it is of limited use unless the Treaty is revised to eliminate or alter the 'nested' central sub-zone (zone 4.4). Applying the formula to ACVs, for example, if NATO enlarged to admit the Visegrad states, the Alliance would either have to reduce its entitlement or find sufficient 'headroom' (the difference between a country's respective entitlement and current holding) to absorb 5,900 ACVs (the total entitlement for these four countries), or convince them to reduce their forces even further. The entitlement reductions required if NATO is to admit the Visegrad states would also come from Germany, the Netherlands, Belgium, Luxembourg and/or US stationed forces, since these are the NATO states in the central zone with the Visegrad four. The ACV entitlements, holdings and 'headroom' for these NATO states are as follows:[30]

State	Entitlement	1996 Holding	Available 'Headroom'
Belgium	1,099	704	395
Netherlands	1,080	1,002	78
Germany	3,446	2,622	824
US	5,372	2,181	3,191
Total Available			**4,488**

Even this method would require an additional reduction of 1,400 ACVs from the Visegrad states or the current NATO members. It currently appears very unlikely that the four NATO states affected would embrace such a proposal, as it would dramatically cut their respective entitlements and eliminate any possibility of increasing their forces in future. Another way to assuage Russian concerns over the admission of the Visegrad states, however, might be to incorporate a strict ceiling on 'stationed forces'. This would severely limit the number of forces any other NATO country could station on the territory of a Visegrad state on its entry into the Alliance, and could be presented as either a CFE Treaty amendment or a protocol. NATO could still conduct force-planning operations or even actual exercises on these country's soil as a 'temporary deployment' as described in Article X of the Treaty.

To the south, NATO enlargement may complicate the future of CFE in other ways. States such as Romania argue that their authorised CFE levels following the Budapest negotiations no longer reflect their security requirements. During these discussions, those states sharing a border with NATO – the so-called 'front-line states' – received a disproportionate allocation because of their geographic location. The Romanian Foreign Minister Teodor Melescanu announced that his country accepted this only reluctantly, and continued to adhere to this level following the demise of the Warsaw Pact in the spirit of cooperation with the West. Yet, if NATO expands and Romania is not included from the outset, Romania would have to review its obligations under the Treaty if it is to maintain a proper level of security.[31] While Romanian spokesmen have avoided describing specific threats to their country that would necessitate such a review, they have steadfastly described the Treaty as one of their basic principles for force planning and restructuring, insisting that their country's authorised TLE must be increased. Since 1989, Romanian military leaders have endeavoured to emphasise democratic control of the military, functional compatibility with NATO, professionalism, and a simplified command-and-control structure. Since 1993, a major reorganisation of the Ministry of National Defence and General Staff has taken place, and an Army Corps echelon has been created. Romania devoted roughly 10% of its defence budget to destroying surplus equipment during the implementation phase of CFE, and this, coupled with severe economic difficulties, precluded significant investment in new equipment.[32]

Russia's dramatic response to the proposed NATO enlargement, together with its demonstrated military weakness in Chechnya, make it clear that Moscow will continue to see CFE and changes to NATO's existing membership as closely linked. Moscow is unlikely to ignore this issue at the CFE Review Conference. Consequently, Western officials must continue to reiterate their goal of improving the overall security situation on the continent. In that regard, CFE is an effective instrument that encompasses the majority of European states.

During the Review Conference, Moscow may argue that successfully extending CFE would be another reason for slowing the pace of NATO enlargement. Although Russian rhetoric against NATO enlargement and accompanying threats may simply be 'bluster', they cannot be easily dismissed. Western officials must be aware that a 'dialogue of the deaf' may be developing in which blunt Russian warnings about dire consequences, such as the destruction of the CFE Treaty, are answered with cosmetic or technical solutions.

Harmonising the CFE and OSCE Agreements

Article XVIII of the CFE Treaty states that signatories 'shall continue the negotiations on conventional armed forces with the same mandate and with the goal of building on this Treaty'.[33] Agreements concerning CSBMs reached in the Forum for Security Cooperation (FSC) of the OSCE in Europe have created a requirement to seek a 'harmonisation' between the CFE limitations of its 30 signatories and the confidence- and security-building measures of the 53-member OSCE. The Czech Republic, Hungary, Poland and Slovakia in October 1992 initially proposed that national force levels be created for non-CFE states, primarily the former neutral and non-aligned states – Switzerland, Sweden, Finland, Austria and the states of the former Yugoslavia. These might in practice be simply a declaration of current levels, with no need for reductions. These states would then be subject to the CFE verification and inspection regime, a process to categorise new equipment, and an annual exchange of information.[34] Those states currently participating in the CFE Treaty would be required to notify the non-CFE states of their residual force levels.

Russia and France have also supported 'harmonisation'. French support is consistent with its Pan-European Security Treaty (PEST), but so far the non-CFE states have shown little interest. This may be due to the fact, as previously suggested, that arms control is primarily a means of reducing tensions between states. It has little chance of success when states are engaged in warfare, and has little meaning or momentum when they enjoy good relations. The Swiss have openly questioned the value of such an agreement, and including Serbia in such an accord was extremely unlikely before the signing of the Dayton Agreement. Efforts to include the neutral countries in a 'harmonised agreement' are further complicated by the nature of their militaries and their views on deterrence. Many of these countries depend heavily on reserve forces and militias for their defence. A verification regime that included a detailed transfer of information on mobilisation procedures, depot locations, and restrictions on the activities of these forces would be construed by experts in these countries as harmful to their national security.

Proponents of harmonisation argue that it addresses the changed European environment in which the major threat is no longer an attack by the Warsaw Pact, but rather regional conflicts, such as that in the former Yugoslavia. But, at a fundamental level, there are serious implications for the West, beyond arms control, that must be considered. At its ultimate extreme, 'harmonisation' implies transforming the OSCE into a regional organisation to coordinate security activities on the European continent, logically placing NATO in a subordinate role. This may in fact be desirable and has been promoted by some European officials. French experts, for example, have supported this approach to 'establish the structures and procedures that are required to allow Europeans to act autonomously if necessary'.[35] Paris, however, might modify its position, based on either its decision to re-enter the NATO military command structure, or on developments in the European Union towards creating a Common Foreign and Security Policy (CFSP). Former Russian Foreign Minister Kozyrev also proposed converting the OSCE into a fully-fledged international organisation with 'a genuine division of labour between the CIS, NATO, European Union, NACC and WEU, with the OSCE playing a coordinating role'.[36] This idea continues to be popular in Moscow, even after Kozyrev's departure from the Foreign Ministry.

Such a development would, however, reduce the role of the United States in European security and could allow the Russian Federation to promote the CIS as a regional organisation while undermining NATO. It would also legitimise Russian efforts to reassert a degree of autonomy over the former states of the Soviet Union, which would be inimical to Western interests and inconsistent with a desire to maintain NATO leadership in European security.

In response to this proposal, the OSCE is finalising an agreed framework document of principles that apply to arms control in all areas to address the diverse challenges and risks to security in Europe. It seeks to provide a basis for enhanced security, enable OSCE members to address specific security problems, create a web of interlocking and reinforcing agreements, establish general goals and objectives for European arms-control efforts, and provide overall structural coherence between existing and future agreements. As such, the framework elicits the support of all states to comply fully with existing agreements, as well as the CSBM regime. In addition, the document also states that the following principles should be applied for future negotiations: sufficiency (so that no individual state can jeopardise security); a commitment to transparency through information exchanges; intrusive verification; and a willingness to accept limitations on forces.[37] In the absence of total harmonisation, this framework would be an effective compromise, indicating that the West is prepared to consider the Russian–French proposal, and even to move slowly in that direction while not diminishing the role of NATO.

A Process for the Future
The May 1996 CFE Review Conference is unlikely to find solutions to all of these problems during its two-week meeting. What may be more important is for NATO countries to agree upon a *process* that will allow all aspects of these questions to be fully discussed once the Conference concludes. Such a process would demonstrate a willingness on the part of the West to respond to the concerns, principally of the Russian Federation, about how the Treaty might be 'modernised'. It would advance the idea of using CFE in a dynamic fashion to meet the newly emerging European security architecture while attempting to shift the focus from confrontation to cooperation.

There are many reasons why this process should not be labelled a 'negotiation' or formal 'mandate talks'. To do so would be at best premature and might also hold back actual progress. Article XVI of the CFE Treaty established the Joint Consultative Group which, as discussed above, performed well during the implementation period to address questions relating to compliance. Article XVI further states, however, that the JCG should:

- consider and, if possible, agree on measures to enhance the viability and effectiveness of this Treaty;
- consider, upon the request of any State Party, any matter that a State Party wishes to propose for examination by any conference; and
- consider matters of dispute arising out of the implementation of this Treaty.[38]

Maintaining the JCG for this purpose, as well as for other tasks – such as updating the equipment listed in the Protocol on Existing Types of Equipment – would therefore seem appropriate. The Review Conference could then examine questions of implementation while establishing a list of important issues for the JCG to address in its aftermath.

Procedurally, the JCG could adopt a method successfully used during implementation. This involved establishing working groups of representatives of those countries specifically interested in the measure being discussed. The working group would then report back to a full JCG meeting at a later date. For example, the working group that would examine the flank question would include the states contained in the flank area – Norway, Russia, Ukraine, Moldova, Romania, Bulgaria, Greece, Turkey, Georgia, Armenia and Azerbaijan – as well as the United States and others. As a result, national issues relating to the problem could be directly aired in a forum involving all interested parties.

Regional Arms-Control Tables
Many states have shown interest in either building on previous agreements or using the concepts applied in the CFE Treaty or current CSBMs to reduce tensions in particular areas. In Europe, this suggestion was first made in 1993 as part of an initiative led by Hungary for the former Yugoslavia.[39] Others have recommended it for the Black Sea or Baltic states because of their concerns over Russian forces stationed in the Leningrad Military District and Kaliningrad. Certain basic principles are relevant, particularly if an arms-control 'package' is to be applied to a region that has experienced recent conflict, such as the former Yugoslavia:

- All objectives must be clearly defined.
- The 'Code of Conduct' agreed at the 1994 OSCE Budapest

Summit is to be accepted as the standard for the conduct of military forces.

- Arms-control 'packages' must complement any peace plan and a synergy must exist between cease-fires, CSBMs and any disarmament measures.
- All parties involved must be full and willing participants.
- Careful consideration must be given to delineating the 'sub-region' to ensure that the security of countries adjacent to it that are not party to the agreement is not compromised.
- All plans must be implemented within the framework of an appropriate institution, such as the UN or NATO.

Normally, a phased approach would be appropriate, with different measures taking effect at different times. Initially 'transparency measures', such as the Treaty on Open Skies, should be applied, to be followed by constraints on military activities, notification of exercises, contacts between military forces, and so on. Once this has been accomplished, 'hard measures' to limit manpower, heavy equipment or weapons, control the electronic spectrum, clear mine-fields, and introduce basing constraints to reduce possibility of future offensive action by either side can be discussed. Overall, such an approach, while compatible with the proposed arms-control framework, should ensure continued compliance with existing agreements and that any resulting arrangement is consistent with them.

Sub-regional Arms Control in Europe
The CFE Treaty provided stability with reduced force levels and the assurance that neither bloc could conduct a surprise attack. Through its 'nested approach' of sub-zones, it further helped to lessen the dramatic force presence on the inter-German border. While the Treaty still has enormous relevance for the developing European security structure, other problems may now be taking centre stage. As previously mentioned, the OSCE's Forum for Security Cooperation in Europe is preparing a framework for arms control, and sub-regional arms control may be an appropriate response for potential areas of tension, particularly in the Baltics and the Balkans. For these localised efforts to succeed, their objectives must be clearly defined. Such goals will vary significantly depending on whether an agreement is to assist in conflict prevention or is part of overall conflict resolution – for example,

the Dayton Agreement. Regional initiatives must reflect local sources of conflict, follow basic principles, and be integrated with other efforts aimed at crisis prevention and management. The general structural outline provided by the CFE Treaty, associated definitions and existing CSBMs, are a starting-point; and several interesting initiatives have already been suggested or even begun.

In the Baltics, efforts should focus on conflict prevention and the likelihood that these countries will not be included in any initial NATO enlargement. A regional initiative should assuage security concerns and prevent crises. For example, several countries have expressed concern about the large concentration of Russian forces in the Kaliningrad area and Kola peninsula.[40] Furthermore, all countries in this region are concerned that the possible elimination of the CFE flank limits might result in significantly larger Russian forces in the Leningrad Military District.

Thus, the initial point of departure in the Baltics must be adherence to ongoing CSBMs and to CFE. Any modification to the CFE flank limits must take into consideration the specific concerns of the countries in the region that are not currently signatories (all of the Baltic states, Sweden and Finland). This could be accomplished by focusing the effort initially on enhanced transparency measures among Russia and the Baltic states. Agreements on exchanging information on the size and disposition of forces beyond the requirements outlined in the Vienna Document of CSBMs, military contacts, and observation of exercises could be valuable. Creating an 'open skies' regime covering only the Baltic region would also offer states expanded transparency and might be more easily accepted by the Russian Federation than the Treaty on Open Skies since it would not include all the Federation' territory.

Similarly, the Balkans outside the former Yugoslavia might also benefit from sub-regional efforts. Some modest agreements have already been reached that could act as a basis for further efforts. Hungary and Romania established a 'hot-line' between their respective capitals in June 1995 and conducted bilateral exercises.[41] They have also established an 'open skies' regime covering their airspace. Bulgaria has signed bilateral agreements with Turkey – the Edirne Document – and Greece – known as the Athens Document. Both of these accords establish lower thresholds than the agreed CSBMs for notifying and observing exercises. The countries involved further agree not to conduct military exercises in their adjoining border areas.[42] At the South Balkan Defence Ministerial Meeting in Albania in April 1996, US Secretary of Defense Perry also proposed further efforts in the region to enhance openness and transparency.[43] These measures will be further enhanced if the Dayton Agreement is successful.

Regional naval agreements could also be usefully applied in the Baltic or Black Seas. While such agreements clearly have their own special sensitivity, cooperation in this field could enhance regional security and serve as a valuable 'testing ground' for use elsewhere. Discussion, at least among the region's nations under the auspices of the OSCE, would further underscore the defensive, non-threatening nature of such accords. The experience of the United States and former Soviet Union in reaching the 1972 Incidents at Sea Agreement and 1989 Agreement on the Prevention of Dangerous Military Activities might be extremely useful in this regard. These are, in essence, a series of naval confidence-building measures.[44] Other similar measure might include enhanced military-to-military contacts, base visits or doctrinal seminars, as well as the following:

- Arranging for notification of naval exercises and operations undertaken by the states party to the agreement. This could include invitations to all OSCE participants to pre-announce their naval activities in the Baltic or Black Seas.
- Inviting regional states (and other OSCE states) to observe or participate in exercises and military activities in the region.
- Establishing ship-to-ship and ship-to-shore communication systems to ensure transparency and rapid contact between the vessels of neighbouring states.
- Closer cooperation in sea-rescue operations in the region of application.
- Participating in environmental protection projects for both the Black and Baltic Seas.
- Enhanced mechanisms to prevent incidents related to naval activities in the Baltic Sea.

Measures of this type could also prevent potential crises, like that between Greece and Turkey in the Aegean Sea in early 1996.

The General Framework Agreement for Peace in Bosnia
The Dayton Agreement, initialled on 21 November 1995, includes ambitious arms-control and confidence-building proposals for the

signatories under the terms of Annex 1B, Agreement on Regional Stabilisation. Article II required states to begin CSBM negotiations within seven days of the Agreement's entry into force. Under Article III, states also agreed to accept restrictions on importing light arms for 90 days and heavier weapons for 180 days and, under Article IV, to begin negotiations within 30 days to establish reduced levels of armament and military manpower. This part of the accord is to be completed within 180 days – that is, by 11 June 1996. Finally, the accord calls for subsequent negotiations to establish a regional balance in and around the former Yugoslavia. Such discussions would include other parties such as Slovenia, Hungary, Austria, Albania, Bulgaria and the Former Yugoslav Republic of Macedonia (FYROM) and would be conducted under the auspices of the OSCE.[45]

As NATO prepared to deploy its Peace Implementation Force (IFOR) to the former Yugoslavia in late autumn 1995, some of the arms-control measures outlined under the CFE Treaty and the CSBMs came into play. Six CFE inspections were made of US

Table 3: Agreement of Confidence- and Security-Building Measures in Bosnia and Herzegovina

- Exchange of military information
- Notification of changes in command structure or equipment holdings*
- Risk reduction*
- Notification, observation and constraints on military activities
- Deployment restrictions and exercises in certain geographic areas
- Restraints on the reintroduction of foreign forces
- Withdrawal of heavy weapons and forces to designated areas
- Restrictions on the location of heavy weapons
- Notification of the disbandment of special operations forces
- Information and monitoring of weapons manufacturing capabilities
- Programme of military contacts and cooperation
- Principles governing non-proliferation*
- Verification and inspection regime*
- Communications*
- Implementation assessment*

Note: *Areas that are an expansion of Annex 1B of the Dayton Agreement.

forces preparing for deployment. Since the number of NATO troops involved exceeded 13,000, all signatories to the Vienna Document had to be informed as required by the appropriate CSBM. Twenty-two inspectors – primarily from Central and East European countries – observed the operation at deployment sites in Hungary. Arrangements were also made to conduct OSCE inspections under the terms of the Vienna Document in Bosnia later in 1996.

Perhaps surprisingly, the parties to the Dayton accord did reach agreement on a package of CSBMs by the 26 January 1996 deadline. This package uses existing CSBMs as a model and was designed to be effective upon signature. The agreement included 15 measures (see Table 3) that exceeded those proposed in Annex 1B of the Agreement.

Ambassador Istvan Gyarmati, OSCE Chairman for this effort, termed the Dayton Agreement a 'substantial package of measures that provide for regular close cooperation which will lead to increased stability'. He also described it as 'the first time in history that former warring parties switched from war to arms control within weeks'.[46] Practice inspections in accordance with this CSBM package began in the middle of March 1996, led by French, German and US military officials, with the intention of eventually transferring their implementation solely to the parties involved.[47]

All the states of the former Yugoslavia would also be subject to the CSBMs listed in Vienna Documents 1990–94 as well as other agreements when they join the OSCE. This is currently forestalled over problems involving the readmission of Serbia, which was suspended from OSCE membership in July 1992. Many Western states, led by the United States, insist that Serbia must enter the OSCE under the same conditions as any other state and cannot simply retake a position held by Yugoslavia prior to the conflict. In addition, the Belgrade government must demonstrate a good-faith effort to solve many of the difficulties involving minorities in Kosovo and recognise all of the Yugoslavian successor states as free and independent.

While success in achieving a CSBM agreement is significant, final settlement of the Article IV arms control and reduction accord will be much more difficult. If the states parties have not agreed to numerical limits within the prescribed 180 days – by 11 June 1996 – limits will apply using a '5:2:2 ratio'. This is based on the approximate population of the respective states and takes as a baseline the holdings of the Federal Republic of Yugoslavia (FRY). The FRY will be allowed 75% of the baseline, the Republic of Croatia 30%

and Bosnia and Herzegovina 30%. The allocation for Bosnia and Herzegovina will be divided between the component entities in the ratio of two for the Federation of Bosnia and Herzegovina and one for the Republika Srpska.[48]

Completion of this effort, however, depends largely on the outcome in the other areas of the accord and the emerging political climate between the former warring parties. If IFOR fails to implement the physical movement of forces required, or if the agreement to conduct elections is breached, these negotiations would be rendered useless. The discussions had the advantage of using the CFE Treaty model, and were also supported by the Contact Group, as well as the OSCE. In fact, this part of the Dayton Agreement combines aspects of both consensual arms control and dictated disarmament, which may suggest inherent obstacles to successful discussions. The disarmament perspective stems from the need for the Contact Group to pressure the participants to begin the discussions, and additional coercion could well be required during actual Treaty implementation. By using the CFE model, however, the discussions did avoid certain pitfalls, such as attempting initially to limit manpower (as occurred in MBFR). The states undertook an initial exchange of data, and a draft treaty was prepared by March 1996.[49]

There is real concern, however, that the parties will be unable to achieve an agreement or, if they do, that it will be flawed for several reasons. If, for example, the baseline approach is adopted (or enforced), the FRY would be required to decrease its holdings by 25%. Current equipment held by the FRY military includes the following total TLE:[50]

Tanks	Artillery	ACVs	Combat Hel	Combat Ac
639	1629	629	110	207

Consequently, the required reductions for Serbia would be:

Tanks	Artillery	ACVs	Combat Hel	Combat Ac
160	407	157	27	5

Croatia would also be required to make reductions to achieve the baseline, but this would be mainly in artillery. Just as in the CFE Treaty, the disposition of this excess equipment is key to any agreement. If the new treaty requires the TLE to be destroyed, then the methods of doing so must be clearly articulated, as well as the verification procedures. The time allocated to the Serbs, in particular, to accomplish the disposition, and whether or not they can 'cascade' equipment to the Republika Srpska, must also be established. Serbian willingness to undertake such sizeable reductions while leaving their patron weakened is doubtful.

Adopting the 2:1 ratio within the Federation would also give the Federation forces a 2:1 advantage in military equipment over the Republika Srpska. This would clearly make Srpska more dependent than ever on the FRY, which may be undesirable.[51] This part of the agreement also depends on whether the Muslim government and the Croatians can determine how the Federation portion is to be derived.

Furthermore, although the Dayton Agreement uses the CFE Treaty as its model for arms control, it may have ignored certain fundamental realities and differing circumstances. First, the agreement (if achieved) would still permit an uncontrolled build-up of non-CFE TLE, as well as the technological upgrading of existing TLE. The CFE Treaty was designed to restrain two military forces that were structured differently, but that at least enjoyed similar levels of technology. This is not the case among the signatories to the Dayton accord, and the corresponding military balance is much more fragile. The limited geographic area of the former Yugoslavia also reduces potential warning time and, therefore, encourages states to maintain their forces at a high state of readiness.

Second, the plan to assist in training and re-equipping Croat–Muslim Federation forces may undermine such negotiations. The United States has pledged $100m for this purpose and has sought an additional $400m, primarily from moderate Arab states. This has created friction between the US and its European allies who have refused to participate. Russia has also indicated that it will sell arms to the former Yugoslav states, including Serbia.[52] Initial attempts by the US to solicit funds to train and re-equip these forces were unsuccessful. A fund-raising conference held in Ankara in March 1996 only resulted in an additional $2m and was boycotted by Saudi Arabia, but subsequent efforts have raised enough funds for the initiative to begin.[53] The Muslim government of Bosnia may well refuse to endorse any arms-control package without this financial assistance and at least the initial training and equipping of its forces.[54] The build-up to the suggested ratio will also allow the Bosnian government to increase its forces modestly – by about 33 tanks, 32 ACVs, 304 artillery pieces, 25 combat aircraft and 11 helicopters. As a result, all three groups in Bosnia will be allowed attack helicopters – which none has now – and the resulting forces will be more offensively equipped.[55]

Third, the Dayton Agreement makes no mention of the enforcement mechanisms available to the OSCE if an agreement is not reached in the prescribed 180-day period. With the removal of economic sanctions, it is highly unlikely that the OSCE can galvanise support for their reimposition if the talks stalemate or if any state fails to comply with implementation.

Fourth, it may be extremely difficult to limit equipment in paramilitary units that played such a large part in the hostilities.

Finally, as suggested by the OSCE Chairman to the negotiations, this is the first time that warring parties have attempted to create an arms-control regime as part of a peace settlement. Previous success in CFE and CSBMs took place in a political climate that had not experienced direct hostilities and had achieved success in other areas of arms control.

Still, sub-regional approaches, such as the Dayton Agreement, are consistent with Europe's emerging security environment. In fact, the stated objective of Dayton's Article V to conduct negotiations on establishing a regional balance around the former Yugoslavia makes it possible to merge such a future accord with the CFE Treaty. The resulting arrangement would involve the signatories of both treaties, as well as other states – for example, Austria, Slovenia, FYROM and Albania – and could build on the bilateral efforts already begun in the area. Yet the prospects for success in Bosnia appear slight. Enormous problems, such as defining the 'region', the mandate, and the role of the great powers, must be resolved if there is to be any abiding agreement. Furthermore, past accomplishments in the CFE and OSCE processes suggest that improved political relationships are the basis for success in conventional arms control, and confidence-building measures are the first step. The key, therefore, may be to develop an arms-control dialogue in tandem with a more formal peace process, as was attempted in ending the war in Yugoslavia. Neither is likely to achieve decisive results by itself, but together they may create the critical mass necessary for a final settlement.[56] Failure would, however, be a serious setback to ending the Balkan conflict, as well as to success in other sub-regional arms-control efforts.

CONCLUSIONS

This examination of the conventional force reductions in Europe shows that, through history, states have sought to use arms-control negotiations to improve their security, save money (particularly in peacetime), and reduce the potential damage of war. If the initial impetus behind such discussions was a rational evaluation of interest, the final achievement of an agreement was an expression of the political will of the leaders involved. There can be little doubt that the CFE negotiations and the Treaty's final implementation illustrate these two points, but the Western security orientation is shifting from collective defence towards a desired state of collective security. At the same time, the nature of warfare may be changing. For this reason, the character of European arms-control efforts must move towards qualitative aspects and conflict prevention. Conventional arms control may now have shifted from challenging the status quo to locking it in place.

As a result, emerging deterrence strategies focus less on deterring a specific adversary, and more on deterring a 'condition'. This could cause conventional arms control to stagnate as a policy tool in Europe. The NATO democracies will require not only new innovative ideas to avoid this problem, but also a more comprehensive approach that uses conventional arms control and existing agreements appropriately. This approach must reflect the new environment as well as the relationships between diplomacy, defence policy, international institutions, and collective security. It must focus on developing a cooperative relationship with Russia, assisting in the resolution and prevention of conflict, and maintaining NATO unity as a hedge against the future.

The CFE Treaty was certainly valuable in the peaceful resolution of the Cold War. For this reason, its signatories continued the difficult process of implementation even as the Warsaw Pact and Soviet Union dissolved. This was successful because the countries involved attached enormous importance to the accord and were willing to modify it even as implementation began. The new environment demands at least some consideration of modernising if the CFE Treaty is to remain relevant. This should retain the essential aspects of the agreement while being consistent with the trend towards a new security architecture in Europe. However, the treaty system was unable to deal with the most difficult and potentially threatening problem – the flank issue. This was in part due to a belief in the West that the Russian Federation would ultimately either accept the flank limitation or make an adjustment within the 'flexibility of the Treaty'. This judgment proved incorrect. It suggests a misunderstanding of both the dynamics of Russian politics and Moscow's objectives in the North Caucasus. The attempt to find a compromise that continued into spring 1996 may have also damaged alliance unity by drawing the United States increasingly into bilateral discussions with the Russian Federation.

As a result, while there is little argument about the CFE Treaty's contribution as a 'building block for European security', its future is uncertain. Its relevance in future is tied to solving outstanding issues and many newly emerging issues of European security – among them, NATO enlargement, Russian and Turkish policy in the North Caucasus, peacekeeping, and developing a normal relationship between the West and Russia. The Treaty can be 'modernised' to contribute not only to the resolution of these issues, but also to underscore the importance of a more cooperative approach to security. Alternatively, the failure of CFE would encourage increased tensions and stifle new initiatives.

A process for future and eventual 'successful modernisation' may illustrate that cooperation, not confrontation, is a continuing basis for arms control. It would also demonstrate that mutual interest may be a more compelling reason for agreement than the threat of punishment following a Treaty violation. In procedural terms, the Joint Consultative Group was enormously successful in handling the myriad issues that arose during the implementation process. For that reason it should be continued following the May 1996 Review Conference, even though it failed to resolve the flank issue.

In this regard, it is also important to maintain both a short- and a longer-term perspective. The temporary solution adopted by Ukraine and the compromise proposal offered by the Russian Federation are both short-term 'fixes'. The flank zone will be a major point of discussion in the Review Conference, and there should be no doubt that an effort will be made to eliminate Article V from the Treaty. The West's inability to find a compromise satisfactory to all participating nations, as well as their respective parliaments, could ultimately cause the CFE to lapse only a short time after implementation. This would adversely affect both future European security and the prospects for conventional arms control elsewhere. Though solutions to this particular problem are important, a willingness on the part of the West to establish a process to address the continued viability of the Treaty may be of much greater value for the future.

For such a process to be effective in dealing with future issues, it must demonstrate Western support for open and frank discussions of the security concerns of the Russian Federation and others. NATO members will have to agree on what essential aspects of the agreement must be retained. At the very basic level, these aspects include overall limits on equipment for each signatory, information exchanges, and an intrusive verification regime. Retaining some type of flank limitation on Russian forces may also be necessary because of the vast geographic size of the Russian Federation and the concerns of smaller states along its borders. Finally, a means should be established to allow states that are not currently signatories to accede to the Treaty if they so desire. A Western proactive approach that was willing to use aspects of the Treaty to assuage Russian security concerns, sub-regional arrangements, or even discussions of naval CSBMs would illustrate a serious attempt by the Alliance to establish a new relationship with Moscow.

Despite the enormous challenges and changes to the European political system, conventional arms control can be an effective policy tool. In preparing for the future, Western policies must remain consistent with evolving NATO strategy if they are to create consensus in the Alliance. New proposals must use the CFE Treaty and existing CSBMs as their primary point of departure and conform to an emerging environment that focuses on potential sub-regional conflict. Encouraging sub-regional efforts under OSCE auspices is one method, and has the added benefit of expanding the role of that organisation – which is consistent with a cooperative approach and a trend towards collective security.

The West should also be aware that the demands placed on arms control as a tool have expanded from the traditional desire to improve security, save money, and limit damage in war. Aspects of the CFE Treaty have been applied in the UN Register of Conventional Armaments, the Wassenaar Arrangement and the Dayton Agreement. Much can be learned from past efforts, but future success depends on the proper application of arms control coupled with the political willingness of the parties involved to achieve success in the individual circumstances.

In this regard, attempting to use conventional arms control to assist in conflict resolution in Bosnia is of critical importance. The failure of the arms-control portion of the Dayton Agreement would be unfortunate. It would be far more tragic, however, if this caused the countries involved to dismiss altogether the value of an arms-control aspect to conflict resolution.

For the more distant future, it must be remembered that arms-control solutions are only a partial answer to a broader set of questions about the future of the transatlantic relationship. Does the United States wish to continue its role as the leader of NATO? Will the Alliance continue to be the premier security organisation on the European continent? Can a means be found to allow NATO to enlarge without compromising a 'partnership' with Russia? What is NATO's policy towards the assertion by the Russian Federation that Moscow has a pre-eminent role in the security affairs of the former republics of the Soviet Union? Can this be accommodated within a framework of cooperation between the West and Moscow?

The most important question may be whether the NATO states have the political will to deal with these issues collectively. While the transatlantic Alliance has moved forward, the immediate future is clouded by questions about political developments in Russia, the United States and many West European states. But although these are questions of tremendous complexity, seemingly 'tactical' choices may now define their ultimate answers. The United States and its NATO partners won a tremendous victory in the Cold War through their policies and perseverance. Having achieved this success it remains to be seen how they will build on it to achieve a secure and lasting peace in Europe. Conventional arms control is not a panacea for responding to these questions. But, if managed properly, it can contribute to a collective effort to alleviate threats in Europe and complete the transition from the confrontation of the Cold War to an era of cooperation.

Notes

Introduction

[1] As quoted in Jonathan Dean, *Ending Europe's Wars* (New York: The Twentieth Century Fund Press, 1994), p. 306.

[2] Paul F. Herman, Jr, 'Domestic and International Influences on Arms Control Outcomes: the Conventional Armed Forces in Europe Case', paper prepared for the University of Florida Press, Gainesville, FL, 1995.

Chapter I

[1] Sadao Asada, 'The Revolt Against the Washington Treaty – The Imperial Japanese Navy and Naval Limitation, 1921–1927', *Naval War College Review*, vol. 46, no. 2, Spring 1993, pp. 82–95.

[2] For a good discussion of many of these factors, see Ralph A. Hallenbeck and David E. Shaver, *On Disarmament: the Role of Conventional Arms Control in National Security Strategy* (Carlisle, PA: US Army War College, Strategic Studies Institute, 1990), pp. 17–18.

[3] Amos A. Jordan and William J. Taylor, Jr, *American National Security – Policy and Process* (Baltimore, MD: The Johns Hopkins University Press, 1990), p. 543.

[4] Richard Schifter, 'The Conference on Security and Cooperation in Europe: Ancient History or New Opportunities?', *The Washington Quarterly*, vol. 16, no. 4, Autumn 1993, pp. 121–23.

[5] John G. Keliher, *The Negotiations on Mutual and Balanced Force Reductions* (New York: Pergamon Press, 1980), pp. 144–45.

[6] *The North Atlantic Treaty Organization 1949–1989* (Brussels: NATO Information Service, 1989), p. 31.

[7] James R. Golden and Asa A. Clark (eds), *Conventional Deterrence* (Lexington, MA: D. C. Heath and Company, 1984), pp. 30–36.

[8] Keliher, *The Negotiations*, p. 146.

[9] *Ibid.*, p. 148.

[10] North Atlantic Treaty Organization, *NATO Handbook* (Brussels: NATO Information Service, 1992), p. 234.

[11] Schifter, 'The Conference on Security and Cooperation in Europe', p. 123.

[12] United States Arms Control and Disarmament Agency, *Arms Control and Disarmament Agreements – Texts and Histories of the Negotiations* (Washington DC: US Government Printing Office, 1990), pp. 319–20.

[13] Lynn E. Davis, *An Arms Control Strategy for the New Europe* (Santa Monica, CA: RAND Corporation, 1992), p. 14. See also *Vienna Document of the Negotiations on Confidence and Security-Building Measures Convened in Accordance with Relevant Provisions of the Concluding Document of the Vienna Meeting of the Conference on Security and Co-operation in Europe* (Vienna: CSCE, 1984, 1991 and 1994).

[14] Lee Feinstein, 'CFE: Off the Endangered List?', *Arms Control Today*, vol. 23, no. 8, October 1993, p. 3.

[15] As quoted in *ibid.*, pp. 2–3.

[16] NATO Office of Information and Press, 'Basic Fact Sheet – Chronology of Key Arms Control Treaties and Agreements (1963–1994)', NATO Information Service, Brussels, April 1994, pp. 3–5.

[17] For a thorough examination, see US Department of State, *Treaty on

Conventional Armed Forces in Europe (CFE), Treaty Document 102-8 (Washington DC: US Government Printing Office, 1991).
[18] Jonathan Dean, *Ending Europe's Wars* (New York: The Twentieth Century Fund Press, 1994), pp. 300–1.
[19] US Department of State, *Treaty on Open Skies* (Washington DC: US Arms Control and Disarmament Agency, 1992).

Chapter II
[1] NATO, 'Basic Fact Sheet', pp. 2 and 223.
[2] Feinstein, 'CFE: Off the Endangered List?', p. 3.
[3] Valeriy Kovalev, 'Belarus Met Half-Way', *Krasnaya Zvezda*, 28 November 1995.
[4] US Department of State, *Treaty on Conventional Armed Forces in Europe*, p. 223.
[5] Necil Nedimoglu, 'NATO and Partner Countries Cooperate in Implementing CFE Treaty', *NATO Review*, no. 3, June 1994, pp. 18–20. See also 'First Joint Multinational Inspection Under the CFE Treaty', *NATO Press Release*, 16 March 1993, and 'Conventional Arms Control: Third NATO Committee Seminar to Coordinate Verification of Agreements', *Atlantic News*, 16 November 1993.
[6] Daniel Sneider, 'Russia Seeks CFE Changes as Warfare Rages at Border', *Defense News*, vol. 8, no. 30, 2 August 1993, p. 4.
[7] *Foreign Broadcast Information Service Media Analysis*, 'Russia Increasing Pressure to Revise CFE Flank Quotas', 17 November 1993, pp. 2–3.
[8] Ambassador Yuri V. Kostenko, 'Statement to the Joint Consultative Group CFE Treaty', 14 September 1993, pp. 3–4.
[9] Lt-Col. James F. Holcomb, 'The Russian Case for Renegotiation', Central and East European Defense Studies, SHAPE Headquarters, Mons, Belgium, 28 September 1993, pp. 1–2. See also *Foreign Broadcast Information Service*, 'Russia Increasing Pressure to Revise CFE Flank Quotas', 17 November 1993, p. 1.
[10] For a thorough discussion of the doctrine and its implications, see Charles Dick, *The Military Doctrine of the Russian Federation* (Camberley, UK: Royal Military College, Sandhurst, Conflict Studies Research Centre, 1993).
[11] Lt-Col. James F. Holcomb, 'Chief of the Russian General Staff and the CFE Flank Issue', Central and East European Defense Studies, SHAPE Headquarters, Mons, Belgium, 22 April 1994, p. 1.
[12] For a thorough discussion of Russian objections to the flanks, see Colonel General Mikhail Kolesnikov, 'Problems of Flanks and Future of Treaty on Conventional Armed Forces', *Krasnaya Zvezda*, 19 April 1994, pp. 1 and 3.
[13] Jane M. Sharp, 'Russian Perspectives on the Future of Conventional Arms Control', paper presented at King's College London, July 1994, pp. 23–29. See also Celestine Bohlen, 'Russia Says It Needs to Keep More of Its Weapons on Borders', *New York Times*, 3 April 1994, p. 8.
[14] Lt-Gen. Vladimir Zhurbenko, 'Statement to the Joint Consultative Group CFE Treaty', 12 October 1993, p. 4. See also Vyacheslav N. Kulebyakin, 'Statement to the Joint Consultative Group CFE Treaty', 2 November 1993, pp. 2–4.

[15] Lt-Gen. D. K. Karchenko, 'Statement to the Joint Consultative Group CFE Treaty', 15 February 1994, pp. 5–6.

[16] Vyacheslav Kulebyakin, 'Statement to the Joint Consultative Group CFE Treaty', 26 April 1994, p. 2.

[17] 'Russia Chafes at Force Limits', *New York Times*, 16 April 1994, p. A20.

[18] Volodymyr Belayshov, 'Statement to the Joint Consultative Group CFE Treaty', 6 April 1994, pp. 3–5.

[19] James Rupert, 'Yeltsin Cancels Trip to Ukraine for Treaty Signing', *Washington Post*, 3 April 1996, p. 15. See also International Institute for Strategic Studies, *The Military Balance 1994–1995* (London: Brassey's for the IISS, 1994), p. 103.

[20] Lt-Gen. Gennady Gurin, 'Statement to the Joint Consultative Group CFE Treaty', 27 September 1994, p. 2.

[21] 'Presidential Aide Claims CFE Commitments Met', *Moscow Interfax*, 15 November 1995.

[22] Sharp, 'Russian Perspectives', pp. 32–33.

[23] Jane M. Sharp, 'Should the CFE Treaty Be Revised?', paper presented to the Select Committee on Defence, House of Commons, London, 14 June 1994, pp. 8–9.

[24] Ambassador Ole Peter Kolby, 'Statement of the Norwegian Delegation to the Joint Consultative Group CFE Treaty', 9 November 1993; and 'Statement by the Turkish Delegation to the Joint Consultative Group CFE Treaty', 21 September 1993.

[25] Sharp, 'Russian Perspectives', pp. 24–25.

[26] *Ibid.*

[27] Bill Gertz, 'Moscow Losing Control of Army', *Washington Times*, 30 September 1994, p. 1.

[28] John W. Lepingwell, 'The Military and Russian Security Policy', paper presented at the IISS Conference 'Russia and Regional Security', St Petersburg, 27 April 1994, pp. 14–15.

[29] Gertz, 'Moscow Losing Control of Army', p. 1. See also Charles Dick, *The Current State of the Russian Army and its Possible Implications for Politics* (Camberley, UK: Royal Military Academy, Sandhurst, Conflict Studies Research Centre, 1993).

[30] 'Russia and the Flanks Issue', Conflict Studies Research Centre, Royal Military Academy, Sandhurst, Camberley, November 1995, p. 2.

[31] 'Diplomats Continue Efforts to Save CFE Pact', *Agence France Press*, 16 November 1995.

[32] Aleksei Arbatov, 'The West Will not Defend Russia Against the West: the Countries of Eastern Europe are Striving to Join NATO. Why? Against Whom?', *Novoye Vremya*, 26 October 1993, p. 23. For a further elaboration of Russian views, see Alexander J. Motyl, *Russian Security, Neo-imperialism, and the West* (Camberley, UK: Royal Military Academy, Sandhurst, Conflict Studies Research Centre, 1994) pp. 1–8.

[33] Dick, *The Military Doctrine*, p. 12. For the background to the development of the CIS, see Yuriy Ivanov, *The Possibility of Creating Common Defense Organizations within the Commonwealth* (Washington DC: Brookings Institution, 1992).

[34] Maj. Mark Davis, 'Russian Peacemaking Operations in Georgia–Abkhazia', Central and East European Defence Studies,

SHAPE Headquarters, Mons, Belgium, June 1994, pp. 1–3.

[35] International Institute for Strategic Studies, *The Military Balance 1995–1996* (Oxford: Oxford University Press for the IISS, 1995), p. 119.

[36] Maj. Bill Slayton, 'Russia–Azerbaijan Relations Sour', Central and East European Defence Studies, SHAPE Headquarters, Mons, Belgium, February 1995), pp. 1–2. See also Anton Surikov, 'Special Institute Staff Suggests Russia Oppose NATO and the USA', *Segodnya*, 10 October 1995, pp. 1–3.

[37] Elmira Akhmedly, 'The West Has Violated the CFE Treaty – Baku Is Unhappy Over Concessions by the North Atlantic Alliance', *Nezavisimaya Gazeta*, 5 December 1995.

[38] Burkhard Bischof, 'Disarmament Round Achieves Compromise; Deadline for Problem Countries Extended', *Die Presse*, 18 November 1995.

[39] International Institute for Strategic Studies, 'The CFE Treaty: Can It Survive?', *Strategic Comments*, vol. 1, no. 8, 12 October 1995, pp. 1–3.

[40] Mikhail Shevtsov, 'Russian General Says CFE "Nasty Strangulation" of Defense Interests', *Tass*, 6 November 1995, p. 2. See also Mikhail Shevtsov, 'Military Balk at Arms Elimination Commitments of CFE Treaty', *Tass*, 3 November 1995, p. 2.

[41] 'Moscow Says NATO Proposal on Flank Zone Propaganda', *Interfax*, 21 October 1995.

[42] Mariya Katsva, '1996: Disarmament Will Be Difficult', *Moskovskiye Novosti*, 24 December 1995.

[43] Aleksandr Sychev, 'Russia Allowed to Transfer Tanks to Caucasus, but Only as Compensation for NATO's Eastward Expansion', *Izvestiya*, 21 September 1995.

[44] Mensur Akgun, 'Other Face of CFE', *Yen Yuzyil*, 21 November 1995. See also Ugur Akinci, 'US Spin Control Minimises Russian CFE Violation', *Turkish Daily News*, 19 November 1995, p. 2.

Chapter III

[1] US Department of State, *Treaty on Conventional Armed Forces in Europe*, p. 21.

[2] Dorn Crawford, *Conventional Armed Forces in Europe (CFE) – A Review and Update of Key Treaty Elements* (Washington DC: Arms Control and Disarmament Agency, 1995), p. 26. See also 'Russia Misses Arms Treaty Deadline', *Washington Times*, 2 January 1996, p. 9.

[3] Shevtsov, 'Military Balk'. See also 'General Karchenko on Failure to Scrap Military Hardware', *ITAR-TASS*, 30 December 1995.

[4] Dick, *The Military Doctrine*, p. 16.

[5] Mikhail Pogorely, 'Russia's Peacekeeping Activities Are Far from the "Imperial Ambitions" of a Great Power', *Krasnaya Zvezda*, 5 April 1994, pp. 1 and 3.

[6] John M. Goshko, 'Yeltsin Claims Russian Sphere of Influence', *Washington Post*, 27 September 1994, p. A10. See also 'Clinton and Russia', *Wall Street Journal*, 27 September 1994, p. A16.

[7] Stephen Foye, 'Russia and the Near Abroad' *Post-Soviet Prospects*, vol. 3, no. 12, December 1995.

[8] Dmitriy Gornostayev, 'What Did Not Get Into the President's Address', *Rezavisimaya Gazeta*, 28

February 1996, p. 2.

9 James Sherr, *Russia Returns to Europe* (Brussels: NATO Headquarters, April 1994), p. 10. See also Michael Orr, 'Peacekeeping – a New Task for Russian Military Doctrine', *Jane's Intelligence Review*, July 1994, pp. 307–9, and Maxim Shashenkov, 'Russian Peacekeeping in the Near Abroad', *Survival*, vol. 36, no. 3, Autumn 1994, pp. 3–25.

10 Davis, *Russian Peacemaking Operations*, p. 3.

11 Interview with Col. Juris Arness, Chief of Staff, Latvian Armed Forces, Riga, 20 June 1995.

12 Kaa Eneberg, 'Parliament on US–Russian CFE Disagreement' *Dagens Nyheter*, 18 November 1995.

13 Alexei Arbatov, 'NATO and Russia', *Security Dialogue*, vol. 26, no. 2, 1995, p. 146.

14 Dick, *The Military Doctrine*, pp. 6–7 and 14–15. It is worth noting that the Soviets long sought to constrain naval forces and operations against NATO resistance, first in the MBFR negotiations, later in CFE.

15 Richard A. Falkenrath, *Shaping Europe's Military Order* (Cambridge, MA: MIT University Press, 1995), p. 259.

16 *United Nations Register of Conventional Arms* (New York: UN Center for Disarmament Affairs, 1995), pp. 19–20. See also Malcolm Chalmers, *et al.*, *Developing the UN Register of Conventional Arms* (Bradford, UK: Bradford Arms Register Studies, 1993), and Hendrick Wagenmakers, *et al.*, *The United Nations Register of Conventional Arms Whence? Whither?...and Why?* (New York: UN Center for Disarmament Affairs, 1994).

17 'The Wassenaar Arrangement: Fact Sheet', US Department of State, Office of the Undersecretary of State for Arms Control and International Security Affairs, Washington DC, 1996, pp. 1–3.

18 R. Jeffrey Smith, 'Accord on Sale of Arms to Hostile Nations Stalled', *Washington Post*, 9 April 1996, p. 27.

19 Crawford, *Conventional Armed Forces in Europe*, pp. 12–21.

20 Nikolay Slatinski, 'Security of Bulgaria: Regional and European Dimensions', *Bulgarian Military Review*, vol. 2, nos 3–4, Autumn–Winter 1994, pp. 65–66.

21 Harold Orenstein, 'Updated Hungary, Romania, and Bulgaria Profiles, Central and East European Defence Studies, SHAPE Headquarters, Mons, Belgium, January 1996, pp. 15–16

22 'Study on NATO Enlargement', NATO Headquarters, Brussels, September 1995, p. 9.

23 *Ibid.*

24 Alexei Arbatov, *et al.*, 'Russia and NATO', Council on Foreign and Defence Policy, Moscow, 21 June 1995.

25 Alexei Arbatov, 'NATO and Russia', p. 136.

26 Charles Aldinger, 'Russian Defense Chief Warns NATO Not to Expand', *Washington Times*, 5 January 1996, p. 15.

27 Alexander Lyasko, 'Although the Doctrine Is New, It Resembles the Old One', *Pravda*, 29 October 1995, p. 2.

28 'Russia Repeats Threats to Pull Out of CFE Treaty', *Interfax*, 20 November 1995.

29 Arbatov, *et al.*, 'Russia and NATO'.

30 Crawford, *Conventional Armed Forces in Europe* , p. 17.

[31] Teodor Melescanu, 'Romanian Foreign Policy', paper presented at the IISS, London, 20 July 1995.

[32] Brig.-Gen. G. Rotaru, 'Force Structure Planning and the Romanian Armed Forces Reform Process', paper presented at the conference 'Defense Management in Democratic Societies – the Role of Executive Agencies', George C. Marshall European Center for Security Studies, Garmisch, Germany, 17 April 1996.

[33] US Department of State, *Treaty on Conventional Armed Forces in Europe* , p. 242.

[34] John Borawski and Bruce George, 'The CSCE Forum for Security Cooperation' *Arms Control Today*, vol. 23, no. 8, October 1993, pp. 13–14.

[35] Phillipe H. Mallard and Bruno Tertrais, 'France's European Priority', *Joint Forces Quarterly*, no. 5, Summer 1994, pp. 19–21.

[36] Andrei Kozyrev, 'Document 433: Letter of the Minister for Foreign Affairs of the Russian Federation to the Chairman of the CSCE', presented at the CSCE Parliamentary Conference, Vienna, 30 June 1994. See also Alexei Arbatov, *et al.*, 'Russia and NATO', pp. 19 and 24.

[37] 'Framework for OSCE Conventional Arms Control', Organization for Security and Cooperation in Europe, Vienna, 1995.

[38] US Department of State, *Treaty on Conventional Armed Forces in Europe*, Article XVI, p. 19.

[39] Borawski and George, 'The CSCE Forum', p. 14.

[40] Pekka Sivonen, 'On Finnish Regional Security Perceptions', Department of Strategic Studies, National Defense College of Finland, Helsinki, 10 July 1995, pp. 1–2.

[41] Harold Orenstein, 'Hungary Profile', Central and Eastern European Defence Studies, SHAPE Headquarters, Mons, Belgium, 23 January 1996, p. 6.

[42] *Ibid.*, p. 15. See also 'Survey of Regional Agreements on Confidence and Security Building Measures and Arms Control', Organization for Security and Cooperation in Europe, Vienna, 10 July 1995.

[43] US Secretary of Defense William J. Perry, Keynote Address to the South Balkan Defence Ministerial Meeting, Tirana, 1 April 1996. See also Robert Burns, 'Perry Proposes Regional Cooperation in Balkans', *European Stars and Stripes*, 2 April 1996, p. 4.

[44] Cathleen S. Fisher, 'Controlling High-Risk US and Soviet Naval Operations', in Barry M. Blechman, *et al.* (eds), *Naval Arms Control – A Strategic Assessment* (New York: St Martin's Press, 1991), pp. 29–92.

[45] US Department of State, *Text of Dayton Peace Accord, Annex 1B: Agreement on Regional Stabilization* (Washington DC: US Department of State, 1 December 1995), pp. 1–3.

[46] Organization for Security and Cooperation in Europe, 'Parties Sign Agreement of Confidence and Security Building Measures for Bosnia and Herzegovina', OSCE Press Release, Vienna, 26 January 1996, pp. 1–2.

[47] 'All Sides Get Draft of Weapons Treaty', *European Stars and Stripes*, 1 March 1996, p. 4.

[48] US Department of State, *Text of Dayton Peace Accord, Annex 1B*, p. 3.

[49] 'All Sides Get Draft of Weapons Treaty', *European Stars and*

Stripes, 1 March 1996, p. 4.

[50] IISS, *The Military Balance 1995–1996*, pp. 95–96.

[51] Marin Gerskovic, 'Review of the Dayton Accords', Institute for South-Central Europe, Rockville, MD, 1 February 1996, p. 3.

[52] Phillip Smucker, 'Conference in Turkey Further Threatens Peace in Bosnia', *Washington Times*, 15 March 1996, p. 15. See also 'US to Aid Bosnian Army with $100m', *The Independent*, 12 March 1996, p. 10, and Barbara Starr, 'USA Considers $100m Arms Transfer to Bosnia', *Jane's Defence Weekly*, 7 February 1996, p. 3.

[53] Johnathan S. Landay, 'US Plan for a Balance of Power in Bosnia Is Left Out of Kilter', *Christian Science Monitor*, 15 April 1996, p. 6. See also Kelly Couturier, 'Bosnian–Croat Army Has Few Backers', *Washington Post*, 16 March 1996, p. 24.

[54] Muhamed Sacirbey, 'Guns for Peace', *New York Times*, 21 March 1996, p. 2

[55] Johnathan Dean, 'The Dayton Agreement and Disarmament in Yugoslavia', paper presented at the Winston Foundation, Washington DC, 19 January 1996, pp. 3–5.

[56] Ivo H. Daalder, 'The Future of Arms Control', *Survival*, vol. 34, no. 1, Spring 1992, pp. 149–71.